What People Are Saying about the
Writings of E. W. Kenyon and Don Gossett...

E. W. Kenyon's God-given talent to convey truth has never been, in my opinion, equaled.

—*T. L. Osborn*
Founder, Osborn Foundation

Whenever this man of God writes, I read. Don Gossett has an anointing to stir up and enlarge people's lives. My life is one testimony of his powerful and transforming ministry.

—*Dr. Rogé Abergel*
Senior Pastor, International Community Church
Los Angeles, California

Don's teachings from the Word have truly revolutionized and shaped our lives and ministry. The victories and successes we have experienced are largely attributed to his impact on our lives. Don Gossett is truly a spiritual father and a friend to us, and we are eternally grateful to him.

—*Jim and Rosie Parker*
Senior Pastor, Living Word Christian Center
Spokane, Washington

Notes:
The Kenyon writings in this book are copyrighted. All literary rights and copyrights of the works of E. W. Kenyon are held by Kenyon's Gospel Publishing Society, P.O. Box 973, Lynnwood, Washington 98048, United States of America. The writings are used by permission of Kenyon's Gospel Publishing Society. No part of the Kenyon writings may be reproduced without express written permission from the above address.

This book is not intended to provide medical advice or to take the place of medical advice and treatment from your personal physician. Neither the publisher nor the author nor the author's ministry takes any responsibility for any possible consequences from any action taken by any person reading or following the information in this book. If readers are taking prescription medications, they should consult with their physicians and not take themselves off prescribed medicines without the proper supervision of a physician. Always consult your physician or other qualified health care professional before undertaking any change in your physical regimen, whether fasting, diet, medications, or exercise.

RECEIVING

GOD'S MIRACLES

E. W. KENYON & DON GOSSETT

WHITAKER HOUSE

Unless otherwise indicated, all Scripture quotations are taken from the King James Version of the Holy Bible. Scripture quotations marked (NKJV) are taken from the *New King James Version*, © 1979, 1980, 1982, 1984 by Thomas Nelson, Inc. Used by permission. All rights reserved. Scripture quotations marked (NIV) are from the *Holy Bible, New International Version*®, NIV®, © 1973, 1978, 1984 by the International Bible Society. Used by permission of Zondervan. All rights reserved. Scripture quotations marked (ASV) are from the American Standard Edition of the Revised Version of the Holy Bible.
Some definitions of Hebrew and Greek words are taken from *Strong's Exhaustive Concordance*. Some dictionary definitions are taken from *Merriam-Webster's 11th Collegiate Dictionary*.

RECEIVING GOD'S MIRACLES
(previously published as *Keys to Receiving God's Miracles*)

ISBN: 978-1-64123-140-4
eBook ISBN: 978-1-64123-402-7
Printed in the United States of America
© 2018 by Don Gossett

Whitaker House
1030 Hunt Valley Circle
New Kensington, PA 15068
www.whitakerhouse.com

Library of Congress Cataloging-in-Publication Data (Pending)

No part of this book may be reproduced or transmitted in any form or by any means, electronic or mechanical—including photocopying, recording, or by any information storage and retrieval system—without permission in writing from the publisher. Please direct your inquiries to permissionseditor@whitakerhouse.com.

1 2 3 4 5 6 7 8 9 10 11 ⫴ 25 24 23 22 21 20 19 18

CONTENTS

Introduction 9

PART I: KEYS TO FAITH

1. God Is Bigger 15
2. Believing Is Now 18
3. Faith in My Faith 23
4. Are You Shaken by a Bad Report? 27
5. Faith, the Conqueror 32
6. The Lordship of Christ 34
7. The Christ-Dominated Life 37
8. Seeing Yourself in the Word 39
9. The Name Above Every Name 43
10. Some Facts to Face 45
11. Righteousness Restored 50
12. Taking Risks for God 59
13. Nothing Shall Be Impossible unto You 64
14. Are You a Faithful Steward? 66

15. Giving from Within 69
16. Results from Prayer 72
17. While 75
18. In the Secret of His Presence 77
19. Lifting Up Holy Hands in Prayer 80
20. When You Pray 83
21. The Power of Praise 86
22. God Living in Us Now 89

PART II: KEYS TO THE MIRACULOUS

23. Christianity Is a Miracle 93
24. Expect a Miracle Every Day 97
25. The Militant Use of the Name of Jesus 99
26. Is It Wrong? 102
27. The Bolder Your Faith 111
28. Come Boldly unto the Throne of Grace 113
29. The Supernatural 115
30. What Is a Miracle? 117
31. Expect Great Miracles 119
32. Miracle-Minded 121
33. Turning Water into Wine 123
34. Lord, Give Us Bills to Pay 126
35. Don't Say "I Can't" When God Says "You Can" 128

PART III: KEYS TO HEALING

36. Keys to a Long, Satisfying Life 133
37. The Living Word 135

38. Some Facts about Healing 137
39. Three Types of Healing 139
40. Can God Heal? 148
41. Healing Begins in Your Mouth 151
42. Nothing Happened Until I Spoke the Word ... 154
43. The Children's Bread 158
44. After Hands Have Been Laid upon You 160
45. Take Up Thy Bed and Walk 163
46. When Jesus Raised a Boy from the Dead 166
47. Stretching Forth a Withered Hand 170
48. A Thorn Dislodged from a Throat 172
49. Healing a Raging Fever 174
50. Healed of Cancer 177

PART IV: KEYS TO OVERCOMING

51. A Victorious Confession 185
52. Being Independent of Circumstances 187
53. Hallelujah Living 190
54. Tithing Your Miracle 194
55. Thinking Yourself into Success 197
56. Power to Overcome Five Types of Pain 199
57. Overcoming Persecution 204
58. Overcoming Loneliness 210
59. Overcoming Discouragement 213
60. Overcoming Unforgiveness 216
61. The Power of Words of Rebuke 219

62. Don't Beat the Devil Out; Cast Him Out! 223
63. Love Never Fails 226
64. Attempt Great Things for God; Expect Great Things from God 228

About the Authors 232

INTRODUCTION

Recently, in prayer, I asked, "Lord, how can I help believers to receive Your miracles? I've talked to them and read their letters. So many of Your people are hurting. So many believers have unsaved loved ones. Others are stricken with foul diseases, crushed by financial pressures, enduring strife in their marriages, or under some type of satanic attack. How can I help them to receive Your miraculous touch?"

This book is the answer to that prayer.

Several years after Dr. E. W. Kenyon went to be with the Lord, it was my privilege to meet with a group of people who were a part of his church, New Covenant Baptist Church, in Seattle, Washington. One by one, they related to me the wondrous results from Dr. Kenyon's effective healing ministry.

They shared how Dr. Kenyon had taken the lyrics of the old hymn "He Leadeth Me"[1] and adapted it to become "He Healeth Me." These former congregants of Dr. Kenyon recalled how they would sing this song over and over, and how people were healed as they sang this confession of the Word. Here are the lyrics, as Dr. Kenyon had altered them:

---

1. Lyrics by Joseph H. Gilmore (1862) and music by William B. Bradbury (1864).

He Healeth Me

Verse 1
He healeth me, O blessed thought,
What mighty things through Christ are wrought,
Disease and pain have lost their power
And I am healed this very hour.

Chorus
He healeth me, He healeth me,
By His own stripes He healeth me,
In Jesus's name I am set free
For by His stripes He healeth me.

Verse 2
He healeth me, what grace divine,
His very life, thank God, is mine!
His blessed Spirit dwells in me
And makes His Word reality.

Verse 3
He healeth me, the Risen One,
For by His stripes the battle's won,
Disease and sin He put away
And all my burdens bears today.

Verse 4
My lips are filled with praise and song,
For with His strength He makes me strong,
He lives in me, we two are one;
O'er all my foes the victory's won.

It is my privilege, once again, to combine the precious teachings of Dr. Kenyon with my own teaching and experiences in order to share the keys of the Christian life that unlock God's miraculous love and power. For the reader's benefit, the writings of Dr. Kenyon have been signified by his name, while mine are designated by my name.

If Dr. Kenyon and I have had anything in common, it has been the excitement of witnessing God's miraculous hand in powerful works of healing and restoration. These same miracles are available to all believers today if they will devote themselves to learning and practicing these keys of faith and obedience.

—*Don Gossett*

PART I
KEYS TO FAITH

1

GOD IS BIGGER

Don Gossett

If there's one truth you need to keep in mind, it is this: God is bigger than any disease—*even cancer*!

God answers prayer, first of all, because He loves us. However, He also does so to build our faith, as well as the faith of others who hear our miraculous reports. Remember Jesus's instructions: *"Go home to thy friends, and tell them how great things the Lord hath done for thee"* (Mark 5:19).

I am reminded of a wonderful miracle that took place in the Australian outback. I had been invited to minister in the Aborigine village of Fitzroy Crossing by some missionaries there. People had traveled there from all around the outback.

Each morning, we had unforgettable prayer meetings at 5:00 a.m. on the riverbank. Also in attendance was the local crocodile population! These services were like a page out of the book of Acts. Great numbers of people were saved, healed, and delivered from demons in the name of Jesus.

One precious Aborigine lady came forward in the prayer line, and the missionary interpreted that this woman had been given up to die with a cancerous breast, as well as another large tumor in her abdomen. As I looked at this woman, compassion poured through me, and a verse came to my spirit: *"Whatsoever ye shall ask in my name, that will I do, that the Father may be glorified in the Son"* (John 14:13).

I didn't pray powerless words over her cancer. In Jesus's name, I boldly commanded the cancers to die at their roots and declared that the woman was delivered and made whole!

A week later, I had gone on to minister in another village when the missionary from Fitzroy Crossing came with a glorious report. The woman had declared to the missionary, "That man's prayer beat the cancer! Prayer more powerful than cancer!"

These supernatural experiences of answered prayer bring people closer to God Himself. Simply stated, a miracle is the supernatural intervention of God.

A wonderful praise report inspires others to have faith in God, whether it is for salvation, healing, or any other need.

> *They helped every one his neighbour; and every one said to his brother, Be of good courage.* (Isaiah 41:6)

If you are stricken with cancer or any other disease, you may be wondering, *Lord, where is my miracle?* I can prescribe for you the most powerful therapeutic treatment available: the healing power of prayer.

Another miracle story that is a witness to God's love for sick and suffering people occurred in Madras, India, while I was ministering in an open-air crusade with an estimated seventy-five thousand people in attendance. Just before I went to the platform, one of the ushers came to me and said, "Brother Gossett, there's a lady here who must meet you now. She's standing next to the steps with her daughter and granddaughter."

As I greeted them, the woman said, "Mr. Gossett, I've been waiting eight years for this moment to meet you again. That is when I was diagnosed with a critical heart disease and given no hope of survival. I was bedridden and couldn't even feed myself. The doctors declared that there was nothing they could do. Then, they heard about your crusade and asked my family to take me to your services. They carried me to the grounds on a stretcher. I was lying there in the invalid section when you came and prayed for me. Instantly, the Lord raised me up. I stood there, rejoicing with my weeping family! I was praising Jesus with all my renewed strength. Wonderfully, the Lord baptized me in the Holy Spirit!"

That woman had returned to her job in a hospital, where, today, she serves as its administrator!

Don't reports such as that one stir your heart? Even as I write this, I am aware of the presence of the Holy Spirit. It never grows old to hear of God moving among His people.

> *It is of the LORD's mercies that we are not consumed, because his compassions fail not. They are new every morning: great is thy faithfulness.* (Lamentations 3:22–23)

Truly, God is faithful to His Word and to you. He cares about the deepest challenges of your heart.

2

BELIEVING IS NOW

E. W. Kenyon

Believing is the verb form of faith; it is acting on the Word. Believing is acting before God acts. It is having faith that God has already acted before He acts. Believing is an utter abandonment to the Father, and to the lordship of Jesus Christ. It is the utter surrender, if you please, of your reasoning faculties to the Word of God. Believing is the unqualified committal of your entire being to the will of the Father.

Here are some of the things that believing does:

It opens up your entire life to the fullness of the life of God. It gives Christ the first place in your life. It turns your self-life over to the lordship of love, the Jesus kind of love. It is receiving life, health, wisdom, and power from Him. It is unconsciously entering into all He has done and all He is for us. It is being who He says we are. It is arriving at the knowledge that *"he that believeth on me hath…"* (John 6:47). Believing is having; it is possession.

Now, I can say to you, "Believing is being," and you will understand me. Believing the Word of God is the utter denial of the world-mind that rules those around you. It is the denial of the dominion of mortal weakness over you. It is the denial of the weakness of your body, soul, and spirit. It is an affirmation of the strength and health of your body, soul, and spirit. It is the utter denial of fears, doubts, and unhappiness reigning over your life any longer.

Believing is entering into all that our redemption in Christ Jesus means in the mind of the Father. It is a *now* participation in all the fullness of that redemptive work, the healing of our bodies, and the forgiveness of all our mistakes and failures. It is the utter righteousness of God becoming ours.

Believing is the exchange of all that we have been for all that He is. It is the *now* joy in the Holy Spirit. It is freedom from worry. It is Jesus in everything. It is being "*now* blessed" with every kind of spiritual blessing in Christ.

Believing is strength for every emergency, victory in every battle. It is Christ's *now* meeting of every need. It is Jesus's *now* entering and filling our whole being—body, soul, and spirit. It is losing ourselves in His greater Self. It is losing our burdens in His love. It is the end of us and the beginning of Him.

Believing is abundance swallowing up our limitations. It is our leaning back upon His fullness. We are complete in all His completeness. We are satiated with Him. His grace is all we need. We are lost in Him; we are found in Him.

Now, when we lay hands on the sick, it is His hands being laid upon them. When we pray in His name, it is He who is acting.

This is believing.

WHAT IT MEANS TO BELIEVE

It is possible for us to learn the key of believing. Again, the word *believe* is a verb. The word *faith* is a noun. Believing, therefore, is the verb of faith. It is to act. You can't believe without acting.

There is a law that governs believing. In Genesis is found one of the three great Scriptures on which so much of the New Testament is founded.

> [Abraham] *believed in the* LORD; *and* [God] *counted it to him for righteousness.* (Genesis 15:6)

Here, the word "believe" means "to support...to be established...to stand firm." Abraham made an unqualified committal to God. He abandoned himself utterly to God. He gave up all; he had no other help.

We find this illustrated best in the book of Daniel by the Hebrew men Shadrach, Meshach, and Abednego. They would not bow down before King Nebuchadnezzar. Even when the king threatened to have them thrown into a fiery furnace, they were at peace. In their minds, if God rescued them, so be it; if He didn't, they were more than willing to burn in the furnace. They abandoned themselves completely to God. (See Daniel 3:1–30.)

The first step in faith is reaching the place where you abandon all. You cannot trust God with all your heart as long as you are leaning on someone else. If you trust any other, you can't fully trust Him. Faith, like love, demands all. You cannot derive love's best as long as you have any other idol. As long as you trust in self, you cannot trust in God. As long as you are looking elsewhere for help, you are not trusting the Lord absolutely. The law of trust is utter abandonment.

> *That if thou shalt confess with thy mouth the Lord Jesus, and shalt believe in thine heart that God hath raised him from the dead, thou shalt be saved.* (Romans 10:9)

You cannot believe in Jesus until you confess His lordship. It is absolutely impossible. The moment you do, the Lord begins to act. You will find ground on which to stand when you reach the place where you can say, "Lord, I trust You and You alone. If You fail me,

I am doomed." Belief is the ability to say that wholeheartedly, with no mental reservation. Belief is the ability to say, *"I live; yet not I, but Christ liveth in me"* (Galatians 2:20). Then, God can act.

> *Trust in the* LORD *with all thine heart; and lean not unto thine own understanding. In all thy ways acknowledge him, and he shall direct thy paths.* (Proverbs 3:5–6)

You have trusted in everything else. Now, trust in the Lord only. Stop reasoning; stop leaning on your own understanding.

Can God lie? Entrust yourself utterly to Him. God's Word cannot be broken. The man who trusts in the Lord is trusting in the safest bank in the universe. Don't trust in the reasoning of people. If you are going to trust God, abandon yourself utterly to Him. Then, He will say, *"In all thy ways acknowledge [Me]."* Don't make plans without Him. In all your ways, give the Lord His place; yield to His dominance.

You have lacked wisdom; you have tried this and that. Now, go down on your knees and cry, "My Lord, I will recognize Your lordship." You have thought the thing through. You have arrived at the place where you have found you cannot achieve success without God. So, get on your face before Him and say, "Lord, I yield my will, my life, my everything to the lordship of Jesus." *"In all thy ways acknowledge him, and he shall direct thy paths."* Fear Jehovah and depart from everything that is unlike Christ.

> *It shall be health to thy navel, and marrow to thy bones.* (Proverbs 3:8)

This means that He will touch your stomach this very day. He will touch your bones. If you have any disorder, He will heal it now. He will be the very center of your healing, health, and life.

> *He that believeth on me, as the scripture hath said, out of his belly shall flow rivers of living water.* (John 7:38)

When His nature has come in, you have received the very power of God Almighty. I want you to so utterly yield to this life of God in you that you will feel His power in you now. That is reality. *"Greater is he that is in you, than he that is in the world"* (1 John 4:4).

You have tried everything else. Now, let Jesus Christ come into your life. Yield your entire life to Him, and He will take charge.

3

FAITH IN MY FAITH

E. W. Kenyon

So many people have faith in other people's faith but little faith in their own.

God the Father has no favorites. Every child of God has the same legal rights. It is not a lack of faith that keeps us from using the name of Jesus; it is the failure to use our rights and privileges.

Every one of those marvelous statements in the three Gospels where Jesus was challenging people's faith in Himself was not a message to the church but to the Jews. They were an apostate, unbelieving people, but they also were a covenant people. Jesus demanded that they believe in Him as their Messiah. Their healing depended on their faith in Him. When we turn to Paul's epistles, we find no such demands of those who have put their faith in Christ.

Paul said that if the man outside of Christ wants to come into the family, he must believe that Jesus actually died according to Scripture and that God raised Him for his justification. After one has confessed this belief and come into the family of believers, everything belongs to him. You can find no place in Paul's epistles where he urged us to have faith. Why? Because all things are already ours.

At the bank, we need exercise no special faith to believe that money we have deposited is in our account. We need not exercise special faith for money that is in our pocketbook. Everything Christ did is yours. All who believe can write a check on it.

> [Jesus] *his own self bare our sins in his own body on the tree, that we, being dead to sins, should live unto righteousness: by whose stripes ye were healed.* (1 Peter 2:24)

If you were healed by Jesus's stripes, healing belongs to you as much as to the house for which you have the deed. You may not have taken advantage of your warranty deed and lived in your home; you may not have understood that it is yours, but it requires no special faith on your part to take ownership of your house. Your part is to thank the Father for it, and healing is yours.

> *My God shall supply all your need according to his riches in glory by Christ Jesus.* (Philippians 4:19)

No special faith is required. You need only call the Father's attention to your needs and then thank Him for meeting them.

For many years now, I have exercised my rights as a member of God's family, and He has met my needs from one day to the next. When He invites you to come boldly before the throne of grace, it is an invitation to come and make your requests known. Tell Him what is necessary. Sit there for a while in fellowship and express your love to Him.

Everyone who reads this message has the same prayer rights that the apostles John and Peter had. You have the same invitation to come boldly to the throne of grace. You have the same invitation to walk in fellowship with God. No distinction is made. God is rich unto all who take His Son as their Savior. Take what belongs to you and know that *"no word from God shall be void of power"* (Luke 1:37 ASV).

HOW FAITH GROWS

There is but one source of faith: the Word of God. As you read and pore over the Word, your spirit nature feeds upon the faithfulness of God, the Bread of Heaven. Your intellect may not be very fruitful, but your faith will grow and multiply while you feed upon the Word, which is faith's food.

The great men and women of faith have been men and women of the Bible. They have read it incessantly. They have read it continuously. They have read it over and over again. George Müller read the Bible cover to cover twice every year. Parts of it he read every month. He was continuously rereading, meditating, and poring over familiar passages until they became illuminated with new and unfamiliar revelation.

Faith grows when you exercise it. Every time you take a step of faith, your faith grows. Every time you trust God for an impossible thing, your faith grows. In reality, faith deals only with impossibilities. Reason deals with possible things and shows you how to make things come about. But faith swings aside into God and grapples with the impossible, making it possible, making it reality.

God is a faith God, the God of all faith. Therefore, communion and fellowship with Him—intimate relationship with Him—will develop your faith life as nothing else will.

Faithful men and women have always been meditators. They have meditated on God and in God. In the silence, alone with God, they have fathomed the unfathomable; they have reached the unreachable; they have lived among the miracles and wonders of the grace and faith of God. They have stood beside God in their dream lives and seen Him speak a universe into empty space. They have walked with the Man of Galilee in His ministry among the sick and the needy. They have heard Him say, *"Peace, be still"* (Mark 4:39) to the sea, *"Come out of him"* (Luke 4:35) to the demon, and *"According to your faith be it unto you"* (Matthew 9:29) to the sick.

If you dwell on your doubts, you will act doubtfully. If you dwell on your faith, you will act faithfully. If you live in the subterranean caverns of unbelief, the gloom of doubt will hover over you. If you live on the mountain peaks of faith, in the white light of God's glory, your face will be radiant and your voice vibrant, and men and women who live in doubt's dark, unlit street will gather about you for comfort and help and leadership.

4

ARE YOU SHAKEN BY A BAD REPORT?

Don Gossett

Who hath believed our report? (Isaiah 53:1)

Whose report will you believe?

Isaiah asks, in effect, "Whose report do you believe?"

We choose to believe the Lord's good report. We learn to trust God and believe His Word, even in the midst of challenging circumstances. The word of men doesn't change the Word of God, even if it's the word of a doctor or a close relative.

HIS REPORT SAYS I AM FILLED

When I was only seventeen, the Lord visited my life in a glorious all-night encounter. Being inexperienced with the Holy Spirit's deep workings, I was overwhelmed by the presence of God that filled my heart. Naively, I pondered, *Has anything so wonderful ever happened to anyone else? This is so magnificent; it must be like the amazing visitations of God in the lives of people who lived in Bible days!*

That was the night the Lord called me to preach the gospel. I was bubbling over with excitement. I could hardly wait until my father awoke so I could tell him the exciting news. I yearned for his approval of my calling more than anyone else's.

Early the next morning, when I heard my father stirring in the kitchen, I went downstairs to share the good news: "The Lord has called me to the ministry." I had hoped that he would share my unspeakable delight. To my dismay, I received a bad report from him.

"Don," he said, "there's no way you could be a preacher. All your life, you have stammered in conversation—even with just one person. And, son, to be a preacher, you have to do a lot of talking. In no way do I believe you could ever be a minister."

I couldn't deny my lifetime struggle with stuttering. But whose report was I to believe? Not my father's. Humbly, I knew the hand of God was on my life in a significant way!

I chose to believe God's report *"that he counted me faithful, putting me into the ministry"* (1 Timothy 1:12).

> *For though I preach the gospel, I have nothing to glory of: for necessity is laid upon me; yea, woe is unto me, if I preach not the gospel!* (1 Corinthians 9:16)

The word of my earthly father didn't change the Word of my heavenly Father. The Lord gave me the courage to respond to my dad's bad report. I became assured that God's Word was the final and decisive word for my life. It was my first major experience in deciding whose report I would believe.

HIS REPORT SAYS I AM HEALED

Beloved child of God, I understand the challenge in your life concerning health issues. Because you have chosen to believe the

Lord's good report, it doesn't matter what the doctor says, for it is by the stripes of Jesus that we are healed. (See Isaiah 53:5.) Nor does it matter what the medical tests say, for it is by the stripes of Jesus that we are healed. We don't deny that sickness exists; we deny that disease has a right to exist in our bodies. It doesn't matter what our bodies say, because His stripes report that we are healed. That settles the matter.

> *So shall my word be that goeth forth out of my mouth: it shall not return unto me void, but it shall accomplish that which I please, and it shall prosper in the thing whereto I sent it.*
> (Isaiah 55:11)

> *That it might be fulfilled which was spoken by Esaias* [Isaiah] *the prophet, saying,* [Jesus] *Himself took our infirmities, and bare our sicknesses.* (Matthew 8:17)

We have a choice: follow the Word of God or follow our emotions and symptoms. We have a choice: believe and act on the truth or believe and act on the facts of the challenge. We have a choice: life or death, blessing or curse.

As for my personal stance of faith, I choose to say, "I will not faint in this time of adversity, because God is with me. I choose life!"

HIS REPORT SAYS I AM FREE

If you have received a bad report about financial adversity, God has plans for you to overcome your "not enough" lifestyle. Your adverse financial situation is no surprise to Him. He will make a way where there seems to be no way.

> *Blessings shall come on thee, and overtake thee, if thou shalt hearken unto the voice of the* LORD *thy God.*
> (Deuteronomy 28:2)

Jesus said that if you speak to the mountain of debt in your life, it will have to obey you. (See Mark 11:23.) No matter how big your mountain of debt is, it's not bigger than your God!

Are you a tither? The tithe belongs to the Lord, and it is a privilege and an honor to give Him 10 percent of all my income. When you are obedient to tithe, the windows of heaven are opened to you and pour out overflowing blessings of abundance.

> *Will a man rob God? Yet ye have robbed me. But ye say, Wherein have we robbed thee? In tithes and offerings. Ye are cursed with a curse: for ye have robbed me, even this whole nation. Bring ye all the tithes into the storehouse, that there may be meat in mine house, and prove me now herewith, saith the LORD of hosts, if I will not open you the windows of heaven, and pour you out a blessing, that there shall not be room enough to receive it.* (Malachi 3:8–10)

As you give your tithe, you extol the Lord and declare that your financial prosperity is independent of the world's financial system. No matter what the stock market does, your finances are blessed. No matter what the interest rates are, your finances are blessed. No matter what the price of gas is, God will supply all your needs. When you are faithful to revere God by tithing, He will honor you by bringing you abundance and prosperity. Furthermore, you will have the Holy Spirit to lead, guide, and direct you in every financial decision of your life.

HIS REPORT SAYS VICTORY!

If you are in the fight of faith for your wellness, do not weaken or cave in. Victory is the good report of the Lord as you are relentless in your pursuit of total completion and wholeness for your life.

God is not mad at you. No matter how many times you have messed up, even if what you did was really bad, He still loves you.

Even when you make stupid mistakes, He still loves you. When you fail Him, repent. He still loves and forgives you! If your financial difficulties are the result of poor decisions, recommit to His ways. He still promises to deliver, restore, and prosper you as you *"seek...first the kingdom of God, and his righteousness"* (Matthew 6:33). He crowns your life *"with lovingkindness and tender mercies"* (Psalm 103:4).

I am addressing two arenas of your life in which a bad report may have oppressed you: your health and your finances. Whose report will you believe? Let's believe the report of the Lord!

God helps you by His amazing grace to remain steady and unruffled when you face serious health challenges and financial adversity. In John 16:33, Jesus said, *"In the world ye shall have tribulation: but be of good cheer; I have overcome the world."*

And He will help you do the same.

5

FAITH, THE CONQUEROR

E. W. Kenyon

It is said that Jesus never reasoned or laboriously worked out problems, as did Napoleon, Newton, and other great intellectual geniuses. I never knew the reason until lately why Jesus didn't belong to the reason realm. Faith acts in its own domain with a boldness that startles those of us in the realm of reason. When the believer begins to walk by faith, he or she comes into the same realm in which Jesus walked.

Faith doesn't care a thing about what the natural eye can see, what the natural ear can hear, or what the physical body can feel. Faith sees only omnipotence. The natural eye sees the great walls of Jericho and hears the taunting of the enemy. The natural body feels the gnawing pain of cancer. Meanwhile, faith serenely stands by.

Faith says, "Become quiet." Walls are knocked down, demons are defeated, and cancers are healed. One might think that faith is utterly blind to physical conditions. When reason remonstrates with it, faith just smiles and says, *"Peace, be still"* (Mark 4:39).

Faith lifts the believer to God's class of being. Jesus meant it when He said, *"Nothing shall be impossible unto you"* (Matthew 17:20). He was not speaking in hyperbole. It was a sober statement of fact. Faith can conquer even the unconquered millions of India and the hordes of China, laying them at the feet of Jesus.

You see, fallen man has to live in the realm of reason. It can be a difficult thing for those who have been surrounded by the world's mind-set for so long to get the mind of Christ. The mind of Christ is the faith mind. The mind of the world is the reason mind. Faith counts the work as done, even when Satan seems to be in control. Faith sees Satan defeated, even when he is seen ruling in power. Diseases are healed in the mind of faith before the prayer is uttered. Faith moves and acts with the serenity and quietness of God.

Reason is troubled and excited and nervous. Faith stands unmoved. Faith knows that God cannot lie. Faith never argues about it. Faith never mentions it. Faith says, *"Rise, and stand upon thy feet"* (Acts 26:16). Faith sings its anthem of praise before it ever commands the deaf to hear, the lame to walk, or the sick to be healed. Faith stands quiet, enwrapped in the integrity of God.

Beloved, this kind of faith comes from contact with the Father. This kind of faith comes from feeding upon the Word. This kind of faith comes from daring to walk out on the statements of fact in Scripture.

6

THE LORDSHIP OF CHRIST

E. W. Kenyon

Before Jesus was born, Mary, His mother, visited Elizabeth, the mother of John the Baptist. The moment they met, Elizabeth was filled with the Holy Spirit. She lifted her voice and cried, *"Blessed art thou among women, and blessed is the fruit of thy womb. And whence is this to me, that the mother of my Lord should come to me?"* (Luke 1:42–43). Before Jesus was even born, the Holy Spirit enabled Elizabeth to call Him Lord.

In Luke 2, we read the angel's testimony regarding Jesus: *"For unto you is born this day in the city of David a Saviour, which is Christ the Lord"* (verse 11). The angels knew that this child, who lay in a manger dressed in swaddling clothes, was Lord, head of a new people called "the new creation in Christ."

After Jesus's ministry, in which He had proved His lordship, His right of dominion, He died as our substitute. On the third day, when the women went to the tomb, they saw the stone rolled back and an angel sitting upon it. The angel said, *"Fear not ye: for*

I know that ye seek Jesus, which was crucified. He is not here: for he is risen, as he said. Come, see the place where the Lord lay" (Matthew 28:5–6). To these women, He had been "Jesus." Even though some had called Him "Lord" and had given Him reverence and love, they didn't truly know who He was. The angel did. *"Come, see the place where the Lord lay."* He died as Jesus. He rose as the Lord to whom every knee shall bow. (See Romans 10:11; Philippians 2:10.)

> *If thou shalt confess with thy mouth the Lord Jesus, and shalt believe in thine heart that God hath raised him from the dead, thou shalt be saved.* (Romans 10:9)

Here is the door into the church, the family of God. We have served other lords; we have served Satan, the world, and ourselves. Now, as we enter into this new life, we put the crown upon the brow of Jesus and name Him Lord of our lives. Jesus Christ becomes the unseen but ever-present Lord of our inner beings. This is the genius, or the secret, of the church. This is the secret of strength and of an utterly dependent life.

What do we care about the world? What do we care about our circumstances? The great, eternal Son of God is our Lord! He reigns over our lives. He is our sustainer. He is our sustenance. He is the strength of our lives. Of whom shall we be afraid? If He sends us to Africa, we will be as safe in the heart of the jungle as we are in our own living rooms.

You see, this question of trusting in the lordship of Jesus is the most vital of all Christian experiences. When the heart has learned to trust Him as He should be trusted, utterly and without reservation, the Lord throws open the doors of the treasure house of grace. He begs us to enter with boldness and to receive our share of the inheritance of the saints.

Without any doubt, every error that we have ever made was because we failed to recognize His lordship and to take our place under His banner. *"Paul, a servant of Jesus Christ, called to be an apostle"* (Romans 1:1). This opening verse of Romans is one of the most significant in this connection. If you understand the spiritual meaning, you would read it like this: "Paul, the little love slave of Jesus Christ."

Can you see it? Paul, because Christ loved him and gave Himself up for him, returned that love. He was a free man—Christ had set him free—but he deliberately took the place of a "love slave." Because he did this, God permitted this man to enter into the Holy of Holies and to see things so wonderful that it was neither wise nor best for him to share them with others. But, in his writings, Paul did give us a glimpse of the riches of the glories in Christ Jesus.

Through all the sufferings and privations of Paul's life, you can feel the tender solicitude of his Lord. He opened prison doors for him. He stood by his side through the awful storm on board the ship and whispered comfort. He didn't allow the serpent's poisonous bite to harm him. In Rome, He gave him the friendship of the household of Caesar, until, at last, Paul cried, *"I can do all things through Christ which strengtheneth me"* (Philippians 4:13).

Paul's Lord had made him greater than his circumstances. In Ephesians, Paul referred to himself as *"the prisoner of Jesus Christ for you Gentiles"* (Ephesians 3:1). He wouldn't recognize Rome as his jailor, for his Lord was big enough to bring him out of his cell whenever He wished. The jail was Paul's only means of a vacation! It was there, in the quietness of the jail, that he wrote the great epistles that have given us the great church of Jesus Christ. And only when you, too, are alone with Him in the quietness of your own heart will you be able to grasp the significance of His lordship in your life.

If you crown Him as the Lord of your life, you need never worry about your finances or anything else, for you can do *"all things"* in Him and through Him who *"strengtheneth"* you.

7

THE CHRIST-DOMINATED LIFE

E. W. Kenyon

The Christ-dominated life is the only life worth living. No self-dominated life, no world-dominated life, and no man-dominated life has any real value before the Lord.

You may let your friends dominate you; you may let the world dominate you; you may let your inner ego dominate you. You might let some great religious plan or your love for doctrine rule over your life, but that does not mean anything beneficial for the world.

It is the Christ-dominated life—the life in which Christ sits on the throne—that counts.

The first step to having this type of life is to intelligently recognize His lordship. You stop your own efforts to make yourself better. You simply lift up your heart to Him and say, "Master, from this hour, I give You the lordship and dominion over this life of mine. From now on, until I finish the course, You are my Lord and Master."

Oh, how far-reaching this is! How little we know of what this means!

The Spirit, writing through the apostle Paul to the Corinthian church, said, *"No man can say* [truthfully] *that Jesus is the Lord, but by the Holy Ghost"* (1 Corinthians 12:3).

I know this is true. For years, I tried to crown Him Lord, but I could not do it until that morning when the Spirit came in and took up His abode in my body. Then, I yielded my life to the dominion of Jesus. He took a Lord's place over my life. This meant that He had to meet my obligations and supply my needs. He had to be the real head of my life.

I had thought of it, planned on it, and figured on it, but never before had I entered into it. I became, unconsciously, His "love slave."

Because I am His "love slave," it is His business to give me food and clothing and shelter. I gave Him my best to make room for His best. He has a best for every one of us, but as long as I keep my best to myself, I have no room in my life for His best.

Then, as I went on with Him, I made up my mind that my best should be made better for Him. So, I cultivated my best and trained it, so that it might do better service and render greater joy to Him.

When He comes into your life, He does so to take your best and change it into His best. He unites Himself with your self and dominates and rules. Through you, He is able to bless other people, and you yourself are blessed, as well.

Today, I want you to yield your best so that He may touch that best and bless it. Then, your best will be a blessing to the world.

SEEING YOURSELF IN THE WORD

E. W. Kenyon

It can be difficult to get used to God's estimation of us—not a theological estimation, but the estimation given to us by His diagnosis in the Bible—the infallible Word of God.

We are accustomed to thinking of ourselves in the world's language as inferior, unrighteous, weak, or failures. And the world will not let us confess anything else.

When we confess that we are redeemed, reconciled, and the righteousness of God, and that God is our Healer and the strength of our lives, the senses rise in rebellion, saying, "No, that takes you out of our class. You are weak. You are a failure. You have to depend upon the arm of flesh." You will not believe that anyone can live any other way.

Let's look at the Word to see who we really are in Christ.

[God] *hath delivered us from the power of darkness, and hath translated us into the kingdom of his dear Son: in whom we*

> have redemption through his blood, even the forgiveness of sins.   (Colossians 1:13–14)

In this passage, we see that we have been delivered out of the authority of darkness. Satan has no dominion over us. The reason for this is that we are new creations, created in Christ Jesus.

> *Therefore if any man be in Christ, he is a new creature: old things are passed away; behold, all things are become new. And all things are of God.*   (2 Corinthians 5:17–18)

The things that have passed away are weakness, failure, and the dominion of sense knowledge. The new things are the life of God, the righteousness of God, the ability of God, and the love of God. All these have come and taken the place of weakness and failure in us.

Colossians 2:10 declares that *"ye are complete in him."*

John 1:16 says, *"And of his fulness have all we received, and grace for grace."*

We are not poor, weak worms of the dust.

First John 3:2 says, *"Now are we the sons of God."* We are *"then heirs; heirs of God, and joint-heirs with Christ"* (Romans 8:17). We are members of God's own family.

That is our confession. God is our very Father. We are His very sons and daughters. He loves us even as He loved the Lord Jesus. What a testimony of the grace of our Lord!

> *Nevertheless I live; yet not I, but Christ liveth in me.*
> (Galatians 2:20)

This is a statement of fact by the apostle Paul. There was a displacement of himself by Christ. Christ took Paul's place so that, when Paul stood before the Father in prayer, it was as though Christ stood there Himself. When Paul stood before life's circumstances and the forces of the world's power, it was Christ standing there. When Paul was buffeted and bruised and beaten, it was Christ who was receiving the blows. It was Christ who whispered through Jesus's lips, *"Father, forgive them; for they know not what they do"* (Luke 23:34).

In the King James Version of the Bible, Philippians 4:11 says, *"I have learned, in whatsoever state I am, therewith to be content."* A more literal translation, however, would read, "I have learned, in whatsoever state I am, therein to be independent of circumstances." That makes man a victor. Say what you please, this is reality. The world may take your every dollar. The force of circumstances may utterly overwhelm you. Yet, your spirit is triumphant through it all. You say, "I am not dependent upon this or that. My dependence is on the Lord who made heaven and earth."

The omnipotent God is your Father. "I can do all things in Christ, who is my enabling ability!" (See Philippians 4:13.)

You stand in Christ an absolute victor. *"My God shall supply all your need"* (Philippians 4:19).

You are no longer slaves of need and lack. You are sons and daughters of the God of plenty, the God of resources, and the God of grace.

> *Blessed be the God and Father of our Lord Jesus Christ, who hath blessed us with all spiritual blessings in heavenly places in Christ.* (Ephesians 1:3)

You are blessed, and you know you are blessed. You are healed, and you know you are healed. What He declares you are, you are.

When He declares you are justified, you are justified.

When He declares you are righteous, you are righteous.

When He declares you are strong, you are strong.

When He says through the apostle Paul, *"In all these things we are more than conquerors"* (Romans 8:37), He means what He says.

Your heart responds to His Word, and you praise Him.

9

THE NAME ABOVE EVERY NAME

Don Gossett

One of my most fruitful times in ministry was my association with the evangelist T. L. Osborn in Tulsa, Oklahoma. He first invited me to be the afternoon speaker for his meetings in the early 1950s. Later, Osborn invited me to serve as editor of his monthly magazine, *Faith Digest*, which was read in more than six hundred thousand homes worldwide. In the will of God, I accepted his invitation. It proved to be a very rewarding decision.

There is so much I could write about my great esteem for Osborn and the impact he made on the nation. His mammoth crusades have been captured on video, and the testimonies of phenomenal miracles abound.

One of my favorite stories is from Osborn's crusade in Jakarta, Indonesia. About fifty thousand people were gathered on the crusade grounds. When Osborn noticed a crippled man lying helpless on the ground, he asked the ushers to carry the man to the platform. Osborn then addressed the audience, saying, "We have three different religious groups here tonight. We have Muslims,

Buddhists, and Christians. Now, I'm going to demonstrate the difference in these three faiths. I'm going to kneel here and pray for this crippled man in the name of Mohammed."

Osborn knelt beside the man and began speaking. "In the name of Mohammed, I command you to rise and walk." He repeated the words several times. There was no movement in the body of the paralyzed man.

Osborn turned to the crowd and said, "Many of you here tonight are Muslims. You know Mohammed doesn't answer prayer, so, nothing has happened for this man."

Osborn knelt again and, this time, prayed in the name of Buddha. After several minutes of imploring healing in the name of Buddha, he saw no results. Osborn addressed the Buddhists, saying, "You know Buddha doesn't answer prayer, so, no healing has been granted for this man."

Standing again, Osborn spoke to the crowd. "Now, I'm going to pray for this crippled man in the name of Jesus. If He answers, it's because He's been raised from the dead and is alive forevermore."

For the third time, Osborn knelt beside the man. He invoked the name of Jesus for the man to be healed and raised up. Instantly, the man arose and began to walk on the limbs that had been paralyzed for years. The audience applauded and joined Osborn in extolling the Lord Jesus Christ for this awesome miracle.

The next night, the crowd on the crusade grounds doubled. More than one hundred thousand people were in attendance. It was reported that nearly every rickshaw in Jakarta was busy bringing people to the crusade.

I admire the fearless ministry of T. L. Osborn. Teaming with him in Tulsa was a life-transforming experience for me.

I salute Dr. T. L. Osborn. He is a dear friend, a man of God, and a man of excellence. He is my mentor, having demonstrated faith principles that have changed my ministry and life.

10

SOME FACTS TO FACE

E. W. Kenyon

The Word of God, which we call the Bible, is a revelation. It is God speaking to man. It is love seeking the solution for human failure and unhappiness. It is love with a solution for these problems. When you confess Jesus Christ as your Lord and Savior and receive eternal life, you come into God's family; you become the heir of God and a joint-heir with Jesus Christ. Then, you have the legal right to use Jesus's name.

Using Jesus's name gives you authority over the devil and his works. It gives you authority over laws that came into being through sin. It links you up with omnipotence and makes you a member of the family of God. And it protects you from the enemies of your soul, of your body, of your finances, and of your family. You are placed in a position of authority and dominion where God becomes the strength of your life, so that you can take hold of His strength and overcome all weakness.

You can be conscious of His ability in you to make you all that His heart can ask, and you can say, with quiet assurance, "Greater is He that is in me than the forces that surround my life, for it is God who is at work within me now, willing and working His own gracious pleasure. I am a conqueror and a victor!" (See 1 John 4:4; Philippians 2:13.)

You can say with simple quietness, "By His stripes, I am healed. Disease and sickness do not belong in the plan—the blueprints of God's dream for me. Healing, health, and joy are my rightful inheritance." (See 1 Peter 2:24.)

God has no pleasure in lack, poverty, or want. Because of that, I can say, "My every need is supplied. I am blessed with every spiritual blessing in the heavenlies in Christ—not a Christ who is diminished and weakened and stripped of authority and ability, but the Christ who arose from the dead. And the very power that raised Him from the dead is resident in my body."

I have the ability of God. Jesus is my wisdom, and the Father Himself is my righteousness. In the mind of the Father, I am seated with Christ in the highest seat of the heavenlies. I am tied up with eternal success and victory. There is no place for fear and/or weakness, and so I speak with strength and courage and confess that I am who He says I am.

WHAT GOD SAYS ABOUT US

Most of us are what we believe, and most of us believe in what we hear rather than what we read in the Word of God. Some of us believe parts of the Word. Some of us have never made a serious effort to find out what the Word says. Yet, we are continually asking the Author of this Word to bless us, send us money, heal our diseases, bless our loved ones, and shield us from heartaches and sorrows. So few have taken the Word of God seriously. So few have made it the business of their lives to get acquainted with the Word or its Author.

When we hear someone say what God says, we are inclined to think of it as fanaticism. Reason is always fearful of fanaticism. What reason considers to be fanaticism is, in reality, faith in the realm just above reason.

You may be reckoned a fanatic by the "reason people." They weigh everything. They think everything through. They arrive at their conclusions. That is natural, and there is nothing morally wrong with it. But it is not Christianity.

It is not faith, and *"whatsoever is not of faith is sin"* (Romans 14:23). It is not the Word of God. The Word is a revelation of God, and a revelation of God is above human reason.

So, for us to learn the habit of thinking God's thoughts after Him, of saying what God says, would be a climax of faith.

Take, as an illustration, *"Beloved, now we are children of God"* (1 John 3:2 NKJV). You repeat over and over in your heart that you are a child of God.

He says we are *"partakers of the divine nature"* (2 Peter 1:4). He says that *"we have passed from death unto life"* (1 John 3:14). He says He has *"delivered us from the power of darkness, and hath translated us into the kingdom of his dear Son"* (Colossians 1:13). He says, *"Sin shall not have dominion over you"* (Romans 6:14). He says we have been *"made free from sin"* (Romans 6:18). He says, *"By [His] stripes ye were healed"* (1 Peter 2:24).

And yet, you limp with rheumatism. You reason with your tired brain. The pain grows, and reason reasons. Meanwhile, just one look of faith at the Son of God, and your rheumatism would cease to be.

You can reason until fear grasps your soul like a giant and holds you in bondage until doubt is born and grows to the full stature of a tyrant, just because you refuse to say what God says about you.

You have no faith? Scripture says, *"Faith cometh by hearing, and hearing by the word of God"* (Romans 10:17). But Scripture also says, *"Even so faith, if it hath not works, is dead"* (James 2:17). Thus, the result of real faith is acting on what God has spoken. Faith is not something for which you place an order and wait for delivery. Faith is the result of hearing the Word of God and then acting on it. God said you are His son. He said you are redeemed. He said you are healed.

Now, you look up and say, "Father, I thank You that what You say is true."

It doesn't make any difference how you feel about it or what the appearance of things may be.

Remember, Abraham considered his own body, which was as good as dead, and the deadness of Sarah's womb. But, looking unto God, he waxed strong. (See Hebrews 11:8–12.) He counted that God was able to make good anything that He had promised to make good. God made good what He had promised to Abraham, as well as what He had promised through the ages until Jesus came. And now, it is no longer promises that He is making good but declarations of fact.

As you realize the reality of your redemption, your faith looks up and says, "Thank You, Lord." Then, redemption becomes a reality in you. *"For by grace are ye saved"* (Ephesians 2:8), and the moment you look up and say, "Thank You, Lord," you are saved.

The word *"saved"* means "redeemed from spiritual, mental, and physical diseases and infirmities." Notice the tense Peter used when he quoted the promise of Isaiah 53:5 in 1 Peter 2:24: *"By [His] stripes ye were healed."* That tense carries you back to Calvary. That tense nails your diseases to the cross in Christ. That tense absolutely leads you down through the dark regions of the sufferings of that Man until He rose a Victor on resurrection morning.

That phrase, *"Ye were healed,"* leaves your disease in hell, wiped out and destroyed.

You were redeemed. You were healed. You were justified. What you were, you are. You are justified. You are the righteousness of God. You are healed!

Jesus is your rest, your peace, and your victory. If you have Jesus, you have all the rest.

If you have Jesus, you have all that Jesus is, all that Jesus meant, and all that Jesus did. When He says, *"Ye are complete in him"* (Colossians 2:10), and that you are *"filled with all the fulness of God"* (Ephesians 3:19), He means it.

If you are going to let the world's thought and your puny reason brush aside the Word of God, I am sorry for you.

But you say, "See here! I have fiddled along long enough. I have played the baby long enough. What God says I am, I am!"

Not "I will be," not "I may be," not "I shall be," but "I am!"

11

RIGHTEOUSNESS RESTORED

E. W. Kenyon

Universal sin-consciousness is the parent of all the religions of the earth. Man has ever sought to rid himself of the sense of guilt and sin and the fear of the spirit of evil that dominates the very atmosphere of the world. This sin-consciousness was born at the fall. It was manifested in Adam's fear to cover his nakedness.

The revelation of God and the development of that revelation have been to one end: to restore righteousness to mankind. The meaning of righteousness, in this sense, is the ability to stand in the presence of God without a sense of sin, guilt, or inferiority.

It also includes fellowship. When Adam sinned, he instantly lost fellowship with Jehovah and surrendered his ability to approach Him. This sin-consciousness has robbed man of his faith, filling him with a sense of unworthiness that dominates human existence today.

Now we come to the problem this creates.

Has God provided redemption to take away this sin-consciousness and permit mankind to return to His presence and remain there? If God could do that, faith would be restored. Therefore, the great enemy of faith is a sense of unworthiness.

Theology has failed to interpret the plan of redemption in such a manner as to remove this sin-consciousness from the minds of those who accept Christ. In fact, most of the ministers who are classed among the orthodox continually preach sin instead of righteousness, keeping their congregations under constant condemnation rather than leading them out into liberty, where faith can function and thrive.

I have come to see that the basis of real faith is letting the Christian know that righteousness has been restored and that he or she doesn't have to live in sin-consciousness any longer.

THE CRY OF JOB

In Job 33:26, there is a prophecy that is striking. It is a picture of "new birth."

> *He shall pray unto God, and he will be favourable unto him: and he shall see his face with joy: for he will render unto man his righteousness.*

There are a few details to notice here. First, man prays, and God hears his prayer. Second, man sees an expression of joy on God's face, signifying restored fellowship. Third, God restores unto man his righteousness. In these three statements, we have the results of complete redemption.

The book of Romans is a story of how God restored righteousness to us on legal grounds by faith in Jesus Christ. It is the great master drama of humanity.

> *I am not ashamed of the gospel of Christ: for it is the power of God unto salvation to every one that believeth; to the Jew first,*

and also to the Greek. For therein is the righteousness of God revealed from faith to faith: as it is written, The just shall live by faith. (Romans 1:16–17)

This is the righteousness that believers in Christ receive. In the first three chapters of Romans, up to the eighteenth verse of the third chapter, God is demonstrating how both Jew and Gentile have utterly failed to attain a righteousness that would give them a right standing with Him. The apostle Paul concluded the argument with a great indictment: *"There is none righteous, no, not one"* (Romans 3:10). No man has right standing outside of Christ. Paul then laid out fourteen charges against the unregenerate man, not the Christian.

By verse 20, Paul had shown that the Gentiles, not having the law, had failed to attain righteousness with God, just as the Jews, who had the law, had failed likewise.

LEGAL RIGHTEOUSNESS

Then, in Romans 3:21–26, we find out that this righteousness has been restored on legal grounds.

But now the righteousness of God apart from the law is revealed, being witnessed by the Law and the Prophets.
(verse 21)

Notice the expression *"apart from the law."* Independent of the law, a righteousness of God has been manifested, and the law, as well as the prophets, are witnesses to its validity.

Even the righteousness of God which is by faith of Jesus Christ unto all and upon all them that believe: for there is no difference: for all have sinned, and come short of the glory of God; being justified freely by his grace through the redemption that is in Christ Jesus. (verses 22–24)

Even our standing with God is on the ground of faith in Jesus Christ. In other words, God laid upon Jesus our iniquities: *"He hath made him to be sin for us, who knew no sin; that we might be made the righteousness of God in him"* (2 Corinthians 5:21). Jesus was more than a sin offering. He was actually made sin with our sins; He was made unrighteous with our unrighteousness. Then, as our substitute, bearing our sins, He went to the place of suffering, where He left His body. He stayed there until every claim of justice against us had been wiped out, for there was no claim against Him. He was our substitute, taking our place, being made sin with our sin.

He went on to blighting judgment until everything against us had been satisfied. It was deity suffering for humanity. And, being deity, He alone could pay the penalty.

THE SUPREME COURT

When the "Supreme Court of the Universe" declared that what God had wrought in Christ was sufficient—that His sufferings were adequate to meet each and every demand of justice—it declared that Jesus was justified and made righteous. Scripture claims that Jesus was *"justified in the Spirit"* (1 Timothy 3:16) and *"quickened by the Spirit"* (1 Peter 3:18). He was born out of death, so that He is called *"the firstborn from the dead"* (Colossians 1:18).

God laid our sins upon Jesus, who was made to be sin and made to suffer in our stead. When He had met the demands of justice, death could hold Him no longer. He was declared righteous. He was made alive. He became the head of a new creation. Now, when you believe in Jesus Christ as your Savior, God is able to declare you righteous on the grounds of what Jesus did.

There are two phases to this righteousness. First, God declares you righteous. Second, you are made to be righteous. You become a partaker of the divine nature so that you are righteous by nature and righteous by faith.

> [God] *hath made him* [Jesus] *to be sin for us, who knew no sin....* (2 Corinthians 5:21)

Why?

> *...that we might be made the righteousness of God in him.* (verse 21)

MADE RIGHTEOUS

Just as surely as God made Jesus sin, He makes you righteous the moment you accept Him. Let us go back again to Romans 3.

> *Being justified freely by his grace through the redemption that is in Christ Jesus.* (verse 24)

Now, God declares that you were made righteous freely by His grace in the redemption that was in Christ Jesus. He did this *"to declare his righteousness for the remission of sins that are past, through the forbearance of God"* (verse 25).

From the time Adam fell until Jesus hung on the cross, God had been covering sin with the blood of bulls and goats. *To atone* means "to cover." The term *atonement* is never used in connection with the blood of Christ because His blood does not cover; it cleanses.

You do not need to be covered. Under the law, sin was not put away. Sin was not cleansed. It was covered by the blood of bulls and goats. God had been gracious through all the ages. He had been covering sin.

When Jesus was on the cross, God took all of the covered sins and laid them upon Him, along with our sins, so that Jesus became not only our substitute but also the substitute for all who had trusted in the blood of the atoning lamb.

Jesus did this *"to demonstrate at the present time His righteousness, that He might be just and the justifier of the one who has faith in Jesus"* (verse 26 NKJV).

This is perhaps the most difficult passage for us to accept because it declares that God Himself becomes the righteousness of the man who has faith in Jesus.

The moment you accept Jesus Christ as your Savior and confess Him as Lord, God becomes your righteousness. Then, you stand before Him as though your sin had never been. God not only becomes your righteousness, but we find that God also made Jesus to become your righteousness. By your new birth, you have been *"made the righteousness of God in him"* (2 Corinthians 5:21).

A PERFECT REDEMPTION

These are conclusive, absolute statements, and we are confronted with this fact: if God is not able to produce a redemption that will make righteous the man who accepts Christ as his Savior, God's redemption in Christ is not as far-reaching as Satan's power.

Or, in other words, Satan has done something to man greater than God is able to do for man.

We believe that God's redemption absolutely redeems man from Satan's dominion. On the grounds of that redemption, God is able to make man an absolutely new creation, created in Christ Jesus. This new creation is without spot or wrinkle, without condemnation, and without sin. It is the righteousness of God in Christ.

We face this tremendous truth in the presence of the inadequate teachings of our churches in regard to the plan of redemption. Instead of preaching righteousness, too many ministers have been preaching sin. If the man who stands in the pulpit is sin-conscious, he is himself continually asking God to have mercy on him and forgive his sins. He is never free from sin-consciousness. Consequently, when he preaches, it stands out vividly in all he says. He is ever urging his congregation to get right with God. Such ministers are never righteousness-conscious because they do not understand it. They are a great deal better than their preaching. Their preaching is a product of a philosophical theology rather than the simple Bible.

You will pardon me for this. I have been a theologian. I spent a year studying theology. I am one of the few men who have written a complete theology independent of the old theologies, but I have given it all up and come back to the simple Word of God. I see the danger of philosophical conceptions of Jesus Christ, of what He did, and of the Father's mighty work of redemption in Christ. The moment you mix human philosophy with redemption, you poison the whole thing.

Let us believe what God says without diluting it with our own reasoning.

BELIEVE HIS WORD

God declares that He has made us righteous and that we are new creations in Christ Jesus. God Himself did this work, and what God has done stands the test of the "Supreme Court of the Universe."

> [Christ Jesus] *was delivered for our offences, and was raised again for our justification.* (Romans 4:25)

A more literal rendering of this verse would read: "Who was delivered up on account of our trespasses, and was raised because we stand righteous before God."

Jesus was not raised from the dead until He had done that which makes it possible for us to stand righteous in God's presence.

> *Therefore being justified by faith, we have peace with God through our Lord Jesus Christ....* (Romans 5:1)

ACT ON THE WORD

Now, by faith, I can take Jesus Christ as my Lord and my Savior. When I do, I become the righteousness of God in Him. Being made righteous by His grace, I have peace right now, through the Lord Jesus Christ. Then, having been made righteous, having been declared righteous by the "Supreme Court of the Universe," and having this fellowship, which had been broken through the ages, restored, I am filled with the peace of God, *"which passeth all understanding"* (Philippians 4:7). I can stand in the presence of God without any sin-consciousness, without any fear, because *"as he is, so are we in this world"* (1 John 4:17).

He is righteous, and He Himself has made us righteous and declared us righteous. This is the foundation on which faith grows.

When you know this, as the Word of God teaches it, you will step into the Father's presence without any challenge or question in your mind. You will know that *"there is therefore now no condemnation to them which are in Christ Jesus"* (Romans 8:1).

If God has declared you righteous, who can bring a charge against you? There is only one Person in the universe who can bring a charge against you, and that is Jesus. But Jesus will do no such thing because it was He who died for you. He *"...is even at the right hand of God, who also maketh intercession for us"* (Romans 8:34).

Someone may say, "Suppose I sin after all of this?"

> *If any man sin, we have an advocate with the Father, Jesus Christ the righteous.* (1 John 2:1)

He does not want you to sin. However, if you do, and you confess it, He *"is faithful and just to forgive us our sins, and to cleanse us from all unrighteousness"* (1 John 1:9). Then, you are able to stand before Him again, utterly righteous with His own righteousness.

Now, we see the secret, the genius, of Jesus's earth-walk. Jesus had no sense of guilt. He had no sin-consciousness—He felt no need to be loved; He felt no need to have faith—because He and the Father were one in heart and in purpose. Now, you are the same, because you are in Christ. And, if you are in Christ, Satan has no more dominion over you. You are a son or daughter of God Almighty, an heir of God through Christ.

Learn to take your place and enjoy all that belongs to you in Christ.

12

TAKING RISKS FOR GOD

Don Gossett

A minister once gave me this counsel: "Pride is, without doubt, the chief danger as you relate your life story. Pride has ruined many and taken away the power from their ministry. No man can bear witness of Christ and boast of himself at the same time. If the power of the Spirit is not seen in your story, the main reason would be pride." I have taken these words to heart. I soak my spirit in the many Scpirtures warning about pride and lack of humility. With that in mind, I would like to share with you some of the spiritual risks I have taken in my life.

RISK 1: KNOCKING A GUN FROM MY DRUNKEN FATHER'S HAND

When I was sixteen years old, my father returned home after spending several days out on a drunken binge. My mother was incensed when she heard about the evil woman he had been with. Her screaming resulted only in arousing my father's anger to the point that he got his gun and chased her to another part of the house. Now, he was the one screaming at my mother while pressing the gun against her temple. With the gun cocked and his finger in position, he seemed as if he was about to squeeze the trigger. I watched in terror, expecting my mother to drop to the floor at any moment with her brains blown out.

Seeing what was about to happen, I took a dangerous risk and knocked the gun from my father's hand. He and I both plunged onto the floor, trying to retrieve the weapon. Being an athlete, I was quicker than my still-intoxicated father and was able to grab the gun first. I handed it to a cousin who was standing nearby and told him to run into the woods with it.

After my father staggered back to his feet, he turned his wrath on me. His attack was vicious, but I overcame his destructive blows. I put a wrestling hold on him that I had learned in school and took him to the floor. After a struggle, he became subdued, then looked up at me and said, "Quite a man, aren't you, son?" I felt no pride in having overcome my father in that episode. I was just grateful that a disaster had been avoided.

Until that day, I had hated my father. But, on that afternoon, God placed within my heart a simple quest to love my father into the kingdom. Within two years, that quest became a reality. I pass the same challenge on to you. Love your friends and family members into God's kingdom. Dare to take the risk!

RISK 2: PERSUADING MY UNSAVED PARENTS TO GO TO A HEALING MEETING

My mother was in need of miraculous healing. Having just learned that Jesus still heals the sick today, I convinced my parents to accompany me to a meeting where a man of God would pray for my mother's healing. Thank God, that risk was rewarded, and my mother received her healing. That miracle became an invitation from heaven that would influence my entire family, including my alcoholic father, to repent of their sins and receive Christ as Lord and Savior.

I would encourage any of you who need healing to go to a church or a meeting where the sick are prayed for in Jesus's name. It may seem like a risk, as it initially did for me, but God will honor your faith.

> *Pray one for another, that ye may be healed. The effectual fervent prayer of a righteous man availeth much.* (James 5:16)

RISK 3: OBEYING THE LORD'S CALL TO PREACH THE GOSPEL DESPITE A SPEECH IMPEDIMENT

In the months before my father's salvation, I experienced an all-night visitation of the Lord in my bedroom, as I mentioned before. In that vision, God called me to preach the gospel. I was overwhelmed by the presence of God as I responded to this divine calling. I knew that the risk involved would be breaking the news to my father.

At six o'clock the next morning, I heard my father downstairs in the kitchen. When I walked into the room, he was focused on smoking his cigarette. I knew I must speak quickly to inform him of the events of the previous night before he could scorn me. When I told him that God had called me to preach the gospel, he seemed stunned. If I had hit him with a baseball bat, he wouldn't have been more surprised. Immediately, he proceeded to ridicule my announcement: "Son, all your life, you've had trouble speaking. Stuttering and stammering have been your problems. You haven't been able to express yourself to even one person. To be a preacher, you have to be able to speak to crowds of people. No, son, I don't think this is for you at all. You've got to be able to speak clearly to preach. That's not something you can do."

He was right about my inability to speak effectively. It had plagued me all my life.

I was taking a big risk in responding to the Lord's call. With all the courage I could muster, I declared to my father, "The Lord Himself has called me, Dad. I'm going to do what God has assigned me to do!"

Having said those words, I went back upstairs to my bedroom. I felt keen disappointment because of my father's rejection. For me, the decision was very real. I was determined to devote my life to sharing the message of Jesus Christ.

RISK 4: RESPONDING WHEN MY HIGH SCHOOL JOURNALISM TEACHER PREDICTED THAT MY WRITING WOULD SOMEDAY GO ALL OVER THE WORLD

"Don, you have received a gift of writing," my teacher said. "If you will apply yourself and develop this gift, your writing will go all over the world." At sixteen, I didn't have the slightest idea what a "gift of writing" was. But, after my teacher had spoken those prophetic words, I set out to fulfill them. Soon, I began to write articles for the high school newspaper. Later, I wrote articles for a while at Glad Tidings Bible Institute (now Bethany University) in San Francisco. Eventually, I became the editor of the school newspaper.

> *A man's gift maketh room for him, and bringeth him before great men.* (Proverbs 18:16)

This Scripture was beginning to be fulfilled when a national minister read my writing and invited me to become the editor of his international magazine. I would go on to write sixteen books for his ministry. The "gift of writing" brought me before many great men.

After this, I became the editor of T. L. Osborn's *Faith Digest*, a publication that was distributed to six hundred thousand homes all over the world. What had seemed like an enormous risk when my teacher first spoke those words had turned into a reality. Eventually, I began my own ministry. Through it all, writing books and publications has become highly significant in my outreach efforts. Those prophetic words have been fulfilled.

RISK 5: RESPONDING TO THE CALL OF GOD TO BECOME A DAILY RADIO BROADCASTER

I have been involved in daily radio ministry for more than fifty years. Although it may not seem like it now, entering into radio when I did was a huge risk. Weathering the opposition and problems I have encountered has been an unceasing fight of faith.

I had to concern myself with such questions as these: Where will I get the money to pay for the radio time and its accompanying expenses? What if I fail? Will people provide prayer and financial support?

Every day since 1961, my radio ministry has reached the nations. Has it been easy? Never. Has God provided for every need? Yes, indeed. As they did for my Master, *"the common people heard him gladly"* (Mark 12:37). These *"common people"* are the ones God uses to provide the finances to spread the gospel.

13

NOTHING SHALL BE IMPOSSIBLE UNTO YOU

E. W. Kenyon

Now, we are standing in the presence of omnipotence. We are standing where God and humanity touch. We are now where man is to take over the strength of God as God took over the weakness of man. Or, as the apostle Paul wrote,

> And [God] *said unto me, My grace is sufficient for thee: for my strength is made perfect in weakness. Most gladly therefore will I rather glory in my infirmities, that the power of Christ may rest upon me.* (2 Corinthians 12:9)

Here we are, laboring together with Christ. He shares our burdens; we share His strength. He came to our level to lift us to His own, and He has done it. We are now so utterly united with Him, so a part of Him, that Paul could say, "Nevertheless I live; yet not I, but Christ liveth in me" (Galatians 2:20).

Ours is not a problem of faith but a problem of privilege. Jesus has given us a legal right to the use of His name. He has all the authority in heaven and on earth (see Matthew 28:18), and we have the legal right to use His name.

> *Whatsoever ye shall ask in my name, that will I do, that the Father may be glorified in the Son.* (John 14:13)

Jesus wishes that the Father be glorified in Himself, so, He challenges us to use His name to do so. This is the "miracle name," the "wonder name," of Jesus. Can't you see the limitlessness of this life with Him? Can't you see that He meant exactly what He said in Matthew 18:19: *"If two of you shall agree on earth as touching any thing that they shall ask, it shall be done for them of my Father which is in heaven"*?

Prayer, then, becomes the way in which we cooperate with deity. It is not begging or soliciting. It is fellowship. It is carrying out the Father's will. We have taken the place of Jesus to evangelize the world and to make the church see its wonderful privileges in Christ.

Can't you see your ministry? Can't you feel the throb of the heart of God as you read this?

Now you can see why nothing is impossible for you. That financial problem is not as large as it was. That disease is not so formidable. That trouble is not so unconquerable.

Can't you hear Him whispering, *"Fear thou not; for I am with thee"* (Isaiah 41:10)?

14

ARE YOU A FAITHFUL STEWARD?

E. W. Kenyon

The Word tells us much about stewardship. There is a picture of both the unfaithful steward and the faithful one. It may be the stewardship of money, for, as we think of stewardship, this phase invariably comes before our minds. You see, after we have been born from above, God says to us, *"Know ye not that…ye are not your own? For ye are bought with a price"* (1 Corinthians 6:19–20).

And Paul put it beautifully in Romans: *"A servant of Jesus Christ"* (Romans 1:1). Paul did not consider himself a "servant" as we think of the word but as a "love slave." The Greek word he used, *doulos*, means more than merely a purchased slave. It refers to one who is "devoted to another to the disregard of one's own interests." It is someone who serves because love compels him or her to serve. Just as a mother and father become the love slaves of their household, so Paul became the love slave of Jesus. He became a steward. And his vow was to be a faithful steward. His time and his money were no longer his own. He held them in trust. He used them at the direction of the Master.

Many of us say, "I haven't time to go to the prayer meeting. I haven't time to study or to take a correspondence course in the Bible."

You do not know the will of the Father; you have been unable to discover the will of the Master. Now, the will of the Father is shown in the Word. Had we known the Word, we would have known His will, and yet we say we haven't time.

That is the first thing in life: when we learn to put first things first. Then, life becomes successful. Sadly, many of us have been putting secondary things—common things—in the first place.

The most vital thing in the world is to know your Father, to know the Master, and to know how to use the name of Jesus. You are a steward of the things you know. Do you realize that you have the name of Jesus in your care, and that His name has power even today to heal the sick, to save the lost, and to bring life, joy, and gladness to human hearts? And yet, you have never used it! You are perhaps like the one who took his talent and hid it in the earth. (See, for example, Matthew 25:14–30.) You took care of it; you did not lose it, but you never used it.

You are the custodian of influence. Oh, the priceless value of influence!

Going by a tavern the other night, I saw a mother sitting at the bar drinking, while her little girl, not more than five, stood by, looking wistfully up at her. What an influence! The child's dream is now to be just like her mother.

We are stewards of our words and of our influence. What power is enwrapped in a single sentence! Homes are made by a sentence, and just a few words can destroy those very homes.

We are the stewards of our words. They can give life and hope or death and anguish.

We are stewards, and, someday, there will be a time of reckoning when we shall be asked what we have done with our responsibilities. Let us be faithful stewards, giving God His share of our money, our time, our influence, and our priceless words. Let us be faithful stewards of the power invested in the name of Jesus.

15

GIVING FROM WITHIN

Don Gossett

In Luke 11:41, there is a striking translation of the words of Jesus to His disciples: *"Give alms of such things as ye have."* In other words, Jesus wanted them to give to the needy out of the things they had experienced themselves.

There is a maxim about teaching that says, "I cannot lift you beyond my own experience. I cannot feed you what I myself have not experienced in the Word of God."

How did I receive the manifestation of deliverance from the scourge of headaches? Under the searchlight of God's Spirit, He revealed to me that I had grieved the Holy Spirit by possessing a spirit of pride and self-sufficiency. I repented of that sin, and God graciously forgave me, according to His promise in 1 John 1:9: *"If we confess our sins, he is faithful and just to forgive us our sins, and to cleanse us from all unrighteousness."* I was forgiven and cleansed! I began praising the Lord for revealing to me what the hindrances had been to my receiving His healing gift.

Jesus commanded, *"Give alms of such things as ye have."* The measure of my helping those of you afflicted with migraines is the measure of my appropriating His words of healing benefits.

Remember when the disciples asked Jesus what He was going to do to feed the multitudes? He said, *"Give ye them to eat"* (Mark 6:37). When they protested that they had nothing to give them, Jesus then fed the five thousand with five loaves and two fish. (See verses 38–44.) In doing so, He performed one of the most gracious miracles of His wonder-filled life.

The Lord wants you to give to others out of your own inner life, bringing the choice experiences you have had with the Father and sharing them with other people. Remember the law of teaching: You cannot feed others beyond your own victories of receiving from God's Word.

If you have tested the great statements in the epistles and found that they have stood the test, then, out of the fullness of your walk with God, you can feed other people. You can give them the real food of God. Their hungry hearts will turn to the same Scriptures, and they will drink from the same well and feast on the same manna and fellowship with the same Christ.

But if the thing is only a theory with you, then your teaching lacks the vital element that a life truly lived by the Word gives.

I'm telling you of the blessings I have received while seated at the feet of Jesus and studying His Word. My heart burned within me as I walked and talked with the Master, as I pored over His Word.

The grandest miracle I've known personally was to be used of the Lord to win all my family to salvation. What an immense joy! I embraced Acts 16:31: *"Believe on the Lord Jesus Christ, and thou shalt be saved, and thy house."* In sincerity and simplicity, I acted on this promise as an eighteen-year-old. As I lingered in prayer before Him, He gave me directives that I followed. The Lord performed the wondrous miracle, and all my family received Christ as Savior and Lord when I was still eighteen years old.

I am not giving you theories. A theory in the spiritual life is just about the driest, deadest thing you can ever try. When I said you can win your family to Christ, that was not a theory but a blessed reality.

16

RESULTS FROM PRAYER

E. W. Kenyon

There should be schools that teach men and women how to pray.

Praying is more important than preaching. When I say this, I refer to the kind of prayer that interests God in our welfare and brings divine response and bona fide answers.

The foundation of this great country is Christianity. The basis of Christianity is a living religion that is in touch with a living God who hears and answers prayer. Prayer, therefore, is of first importance.

Simply talking off into the air is not praying.

I believe we should pray for results. If we pray and nothing follows, we should seek a remedy to the problem. The big things of Christianity are supernatural, and if supernatural things are not done, it shows that we have the form only without power.

All these things are offered to us through prayer, and if we do not have them, it is because we have not made our prayer connection.

We know that God hears prayer. You know it, and I know it. I have seen thousands of souls saved in answer to prayer. I have seen thousands of dollars come in. I have seen demons cast out and thousands healed of diseases in answer to prayer. I have seen the miraculous power of God manifested hundreds of times.

On the other hand, I have seen churches in which there has not been a soul saved for years—not a sterling example of the power of prayer, and yet they keep on praying with no results!

Is God untrue? Are the days of praying over? Have we promises made by a bankrupt God? Perhaps we are not known in the bank of heaven. We had better get Jesus to introduce us there.

Jesus has given us the power of attorney to use His name in prayer to the Father. *"If ye shall ask any thing in my name, I will do it"* (John 14:14). That's final.

We know that Jesus and the Father entered into a wonderful blood covenant with us, and this alone guarantees us answers to our prayers. Then, Jesus gave us the Great Commission and said He would be with us to the end of the age. (See Matthew 28:18–20.) If He sends us out, He must back us up, for no soldier goes out under his own charge.

Jesus must answer our prayer and meet our needs.

There is great need that is facing us everywhere. Men are dying for need of Christ. The sick need healing and the weak need strength.

Are you doing what He wants you to do?

Is your life right with God?

Does your heart condemn you?

If so, get right with God, now.

Get down on your knees before the Mighty One and believe your way through the hosts of demons who want to hinder your prayers. Pray your way to victory.

If you are praying for the sick, stick to it; don't give up. If you are praying for money, command it loosened in the mighty name of Jesus. If you are praying for souls, stand by until you see the answer.

17

WHILE

E. W. Kenyon

As my heart grows quiet and all the voices in my inner spirit are hushed, a voice comes clearly, saying, *"Seek ye the LORD while he may be found, call ye upon him while he is near"* (Isaiah 55:6).

It is the voice of love.

It is the voice of the strong One, calling the weak ones to walk with Him.

It is the voice of success, calling all us failures to drink at His fountain of victory and joy.

It is the voice of my Father, speaking to the wayward, thoughtless youth—young men and women—calling them out of their bondage of habits and weakness into the realm of liberty, strength, and success.

Oh, so many of us foolishly bind our feet with habits—the feet that must bear us and carry us up that mountain, with all its difficulties and problems, to the highlands of victory. How often we foolishly handicap ourselves! We allow habits to bind our minds and dull our thinking. We allow our minds, the only instruments we have that can make us independent of circumstances and lift us into leadership, to be diseased with wrong thinking, wrong listening, and wrong seeing. Then, out of the fog of blunders and mistakes, we hear His voice, sweetly and clearly. The radio of our souls has picked His voice out of the air, and I hear Him whisper again, *"Seek ye the* LORD *while he may be found."*

My heart lingers over that word *"while."* I know what it means. It means there will come a time when, if you have not named Him Lord and Savior, He will not be found, a time when He will not be "on the air." On that day, if you have yet to bend a knee to His lordship, you will turn the dial of your heart's radio feverishly, but there will be no signal.

God is on the air. Set your dial on Him now.

Men and women, you will never find salvation, you will never receive peace, and you will never be who you were created to be until you link up with God. Take this Man Jesus as your Lord and allow Him to lead you out of the fog banks of failure and fear and into the clear sunlight of victory and joy. He will crown you with success. He will make life worth the living. He will make life big. He will make it a living romance, day by day.

Come, walk with Him while He may be found.

18

IN THE SECRET OF HIS PRESENCE

E. W. Kenyon

There are three prayer problems that I would like to bring to your attention: first, the effective prayer for the salvation of souls; second, the effective prayer for finances; and, third, the sincere bearing of another's burden.

Day after day, we come into contact with a never-ending stream of people. Many of them are restless, unsettled, and searching for something that will satisfy. At times, you can see it in their eyes, hear it in their voices, feel it in their handshakes, or recognize it in the manner of their walk. You hear your neighbors scolding their children and fretting over their behavior. You notice the worn looks on their faces.

All these things are but a manifestation of a deep-seated need for the Son of God, a Savior—a rest, a peace, a strength, and a quietness that they do not have.

In your church services, strangers are constantly coming into your midst. Many of them are unsaved and searching for that "something." Meanwhile, many of your fellow church members are attempting to portray, in an outward way, a life they do not possess inwardly.

Then, from across the waters come calls for help from the mission fields. These heartaches and burdens can be met through prayer alone. God has left everything up to prayer. It is the only channel left.

The man or woman who journeys down into heart-searching prayer is the channel through whom God can work. The one who takes these burdens and bears them to the Lord in prayer is also the one whom God can trust to go and speak the necessary word when the time comes. In other words, the one who prays is a personal worker, and the personal worker is, of necessity, a prayer warrior.

Daily, many are confronted with financial problems. It may be financial need in the home, in the church, or in the mission field. Too often, God's people limp along, skimping a little here and stretching a little there to make both ends meet, while His storehouse is full and running over.

There are avenues of endeavor that would mean carrying God's message of salvation to hundreds of thousands of people. The door is standing wide open, and yet, the church is often too feeble to crawl across the threshold because of its limited resources.

Why? It is only because God's people have failed to pray.

We do not need to ask another to give. We do not need to make public appeals for extra funds by asking others to give. If each person will honestly get down and pray, the money will come. Time and again in our ministry, we have proved this to be true.

Here is the secret: if I am honestly giving all that my Lord expects me to give, I can honestly pray that He will pour out His abundance.

The inward man is conscious of the fact that he cannot hide anything from God. Man may fool his fellow man, but there can be no secrets from the Father. One may rise and publicly address a prayer to the God of the universe, and he may seem spiritual in the eyes of other people, but that man knows in his heart whether God hears him or not.

This is not a matter in which men may judge each other. It is a matter in which each one, in his or her own heart, must judge himself or herself.

Then, there is the third problem: What do you do when someone asks you to pray for him? Have you promised to pray for individuals and then failed to carry out their request? Have you received their requests as a burden and conveyed that trust to the throne of grace? Have you been faithful to those who have entrusted you with their hearts' problems?

The hungry hearts of the unsatisfied are looking to you and expecting results when you pray. The burdened heart of your brother or sister in the Lord expects to feel a lifting of the heart-crushing pressure when you pray.

We must become blood-covenant men and women and dutifully share each others' burdens. Dwell in the Word and become a prayer warrior. Join the prayer ranks. Spend much time in the secret of God's presence, shut away, where only the ear of the Father will hear, and, hearing, He will answer:

> *Call unto me, and I will answer thee, and show thee great and mighty things, which thou knowest not.*   (Jeremiah 33:3)

19

LIFTING UP HOLY HANDS IN PRAYER

Don Gossett

I will therefore that men pray every where, lifting up holy hands, without wrath and doubting. (1 Timothy 2:8)

Being of sound bodies, most of us can freely lift our hands in prayer, thereby obeying this command of the apostle Paul. Jesus said, "With men it is impossible, but not with God: for with God all things are possible" (Mark 10:27). There may be no solution to whatever you are going through, but nothing is too hard for God!

Behold, I am the Lord, the God of all flesh: is there any thing too hard for me? (Jeremiah 32:27)

Call unto me, and I will answer thee, and show thee great and mighty things, which thou knowest not. (Jeremiah 33:3)

No illness is too great.

> [Jesus] *said unto them, They that be whole need not a physician, but they that are sick....And Jesus went about all the cities and villages, teaching in their synagogues, and preaching the gospel of the kingdom, and healing every sickness and every disease among the people.* (Matthew 9:12, 35)

Jesus is the Great Physician, and He still heals people today.

No financial need is too great. I once lost my home and furniture by repossession because I didn't have enough money. But, after I lifted up holy hands in prayer, God gave me a better home than I had had before.

No fear is too great. In 1976, a cancerous growth threatened to cut down my life prematurely. The fears I battled were tormenting. I clung to God's Word. *"I sought the LORD, and he heard me, and delivered me from all my fears"* (Psalm 34:4). Without surgery, that ugly growth was removed from my head through spiritual healing. Praise the Lord!

No person is beyond forgiveness.

No form of loneliness is too overwhelming.

No relationship is too broken.

No loss is too devastating.

Take this truth for yourself: Nothing is too hard for God!

While I was in Beirut, Lebanon, adverse circumstances had left me financially broke, hopeless, and discouraged. Having no funds to rent a room or to buy food frustrated me to the core. I was almost to the point of believing that there was no answer to my dilemma.

At that moment, the eerie wail sounded, calling Muslims to prayer. Luckily, I was ignorant of Muslim laws that forbid Christians from praying at mosques. The only restriction given to me was, "Remove your shoes." In my bare feet, I prayed that day. I devoted an hour to seeking God's help in prayer. Thankfully, the living God, whom I was representing in Beirut, readily and willingly gave me divine help.

Two Arab strangers gave me five hundred U.S. dollars. I received a complimentary room overlooking the ocean. My meals were provided for free. In due time, I was on my way to my next destination. Yes, I had faced insurmountable situations, but I had discovered that, with God, nothing is ever impossible.

Psalm 105:4 carries this instruction: *"Seek the LORD, and his strength: seek his face evermore."* What does it mean to *"seek his face"*? In Scripture, the mention of the face of God is a reference to His manifest presence. When we "seek His face," it means that we desire to have an audience with Him. It's more than a casual contact. When we accept the invitation of Hebrews 4 to *"come boldly unto the throne of grace"* (verse 16), we must understand that we are approaching the holy God and must ascribe to Him the honor, glory, and praise due His holy name.

In Matthew 6, Jesus prefaced His instructions by saying, *"When thou prayest"* (verse 5), not "If thou prayest." There is power in prayer.

I challenge you to *"pray...lifting up holy hands."* Make your requests known to God. There is deliverance through prayer. Forgiveness and peace come through prayer. Help with life's decisions comes through prayer. Healing comes through prayer. Provision for life's basic needs comes through prayer. Restored relationships with God, your spouse, your children, and your coworkers all come through prayer.

20

WHEN YOU PRAY

E. W. Kenyon

You have asked the Father for something in the name of Jesus. Now, you are to act as though you have it. You are to talk as though you possess it. You are never to go back on your prayer. If you have asked someone to pray for you, act as though you possess the thing for which that person prayed. You are never to allow yourself to speak as though you don't have it. You are to know that you have it. You are to thank the Father as though you have it in your possession right now.

Faith is always thankful, always full of praise.

You have asked in Jesus's name, and you are heard. You cannot see the answer, but you know that it has come to pass. You know that your prayer is answered. If there is such a thing as a bookkeeper in heaven, the person who is in charge of that department has put your request down and, opposite it, has written "Answered."

Now, what are you going to do about it? You are going to praise God for it. You are going to thank Him for it.

Likewise, any unbelief in your own prayer, or the prayers of anyone else, can annul that prayer; it can annul faith.

> *Be careful for nothing; but in every thing by prayer and supplication with thanksgiving let your requests be made known unto God.* (Philippians 4:6)

This verse is worthy of our consideration. Notice that we are never to be anxious. After you have prayed, be certain that your prayer was made to the Father in the name of Jesus and that it rested squarely upon His own written Word. Your prayer must be answered unless you annul it yourself, unless you make it void, by your unwise talk of doubts.

We are to pray with thanksgiving. Why shouldn't you be thankful? Did you pray? Yes. Did God hear you? Yes. He heard you if your prayer was according to His will, and we know that He hears us when we pray like that. Thus, what am I going to do about it? I am going to rejoice, waiting for the fulfillment of my prayer. It is as though I owed a bill that I couldn't pay, and someone else paid it and said, "Here is a receipt for that bill."

Then, I ask again, "Did you pay it?" "Yes," he says. "You have the receipt, don't you?" And my heart grows full of laughter because it is done.

Isn't the Father's word as good as that receipt? Isn't the Father's word as good as that man's word? Of course, it is. Then, cast all your anxiety on God because He has answered you.

You see, prayer is done according to His will. You are laboring together with Him. You have made your request known to Him, and it is His work to fulfill it. You are His partner in this work. You have done your part. He has fulfilled His part. Now, *"the peace of God, which passeth all understanding"* (Philippians 4:7) fills your heart because you know your prayer is answered. You can go about your business with a heart full of thanksgiving. You can say,

"Father, I want to thank You because You have heard my prayer and because You have answered it."

The enemy will say, "You have no evidence."

You will reply, "I have evidence. I have the Word of God."

The adversary will say, "But you don't feel it, do you?"

And you will say, "I don't need feeling. I have the Word. I don't need any evidence of the senses to prove that my Father's word is true. No word from God is void of fulfillment."

> *So shall my word be that goeth forth out of my mouth: it shall not return unto me void, but it shall accomplish that which I please, and it shall prosper in the thing whereto I sent it.*
>
> (Isaiah 55:11)

21

THE POWER OF PRAISE

Don Gossett

If you focus your efforts on praising the Lord, God will work mightily in your life. How? In healing powerfully, in providing for your needs, in working changes in the lives of those dearest to you. I am convinced that you can accomplish anything God has called you to do when you daily express your wholehearted praise to the Lord Jesus.

Let me tell you the story of a lady named Ruth who was afflicted with twenty-four diseases. As you might imagine, her condition was rapidly deteriorating. The afflictions in her body had caused her to be keenly sensitive to noises. Unfortunately, the neighborhood where she lived with her husband, Ray, was a noisy one. Ray made a decision to move them to a more quiet, rural location. Ruth's nerves, however, were so damaged that she couldn't stand any kind of sound—voices, music, television, or radio. Finally, her condition deteriorated to the point that she could no longer tolerate even Ray's voice. One morning, Ruth's mother came to visit and whispered, "Ruth, darling, I was in prayer for you this morning. The Lord told me that if you will listen to Brother Don Gossett on the radio today, He will heal you."

Ruth protested, "But, Mother, you know I can't stand to hear a radio broadcast. It would be too painful."

Her mother responded, "The Lord has spoken. Brother Don will have a message for you that the Lord will use in your healing. Please, Ruth, listen to his broadcast with me today."

Of course, I knew nothing about this conversation. God, however, gave me a word of knowledge that day. When I came to the close of my broadcast, I said, "It's time to join me as we praise the Lord ten times. If you are so weak that you can only whisper, go ahead and whisper ten times, 'Praise the Lord.'"

That got Ruth's attention. She whispered to her mother, "He's talking about me. The Lord knows I can only whisper."

Then, Ruth whispered, "Praise the Lord!" ten times.

Ruth felt so uplifted from praising the Lord that she decided to listen to my broadcast again the next morning and the next morning after that. In fact, it soon became an everyday occurrence.

Although it did not happen instantaneously, day by day, Ruth's health was being restored as she praised the Lord. Before long, the twenty-four diseases that had ravaged her body were all healed. The power of the Lord had accomplished the work. Ruth was restored to wonderful health and wholeness.

I first learned of this story when Ray and Ruth came to a meeting I was conducting. Later, they were twice guests on my daily radio broadcast, where Ray shared that for two whole years, he and Ruth spoke to each other only in whispers. Ruth's testimony of the power of expressing "Praise the Lord!" ten times encouraged many sick people to follow the same practice. Her experience has been an inspiration to thousands.

What were the dynamic factors in Ruth's speaking forth, even in a whisper, "Praise the Lord"?

But thou art holy, O thou that inhabitest the praises of Israel.
(Psalm 22:3)

The Lord inhabits our praises. *To inhabit* means "to remain, stay...to dwell, have one's abode." When you say, "Praise the Lord!" you aren't speaking magic words. Since the Lord inhabits our praises, the manifestations of His power to heal and deliver are often the byproducts.

Whoso offereth praise glorifieth me. (Psalm 50:23)

Whenever you offer the Lord genuine, wholehearted vocal praise, you glorify Him! What an awesome privilege!

Because of the power in praising the Lord, our home atmosphere has gone from anger to aroma, from bitter to better, from complaining to contentment, from fear to faith, and from grumbling to gratitude.

22

GOD LIVING IN US NOW

E. W. Kenyon

Christians are born of the Spirit in order to give God a home within their bodies.

The apostle Paul wrote, "*If God be **for** us, who can be against us?*" (Romans 8:31, emphasis added).

Jesus said, "*Lo, I am **with** you alway*" (Matthew 28:20, emphasis added).

Paul also wrote, "*For it is God which worketh **in** you*" (Philippians 2:13, emphasis added).

God is *for* you, *with* you, and *in* you. In response, we ought to become "God-inside-minded."

> *Ye are of God, little children, and have overcome them: because greater is he that is in you, than he that is in the world.*
> (1 John 4:4)

If this "God-inside-mindedness" became a reality to you, you would step out of your weakness and into the fullness of your privileges in Christ. If you have called Jesus Christ your Lord and Savior, you have been born again, that He might dwell in you. You became *"the righteousness of God"* (2 Corinthians 5:21), that He might live in you. You are a member of the body of Christ, to the end that He might dwell in you.

He dwelleth with you, and shall be in you. (John 14:17)

When you awaken in the morning, remember that *"greater is he that is in you"* (1 John 4:4) than anything you will face that day.

The Spirit of Him who raised Jesus from the dead dwells in you. (Romans 8:11 NKJV)

He will heal your mortal body and fill it with resurrection life. (See verse 11.)

What a thrill that is! How wonderful it is that the Spirit who raised Jesus from the dead is in you. Let's return to that verse in Philippians:

For it is God which worketh in you both to will and to do of his good pleasure. (Philippians 2:13)

If you will take the attitude that He is there, He will be there. If your faith insists that He is inside you, He will be there, as sure as God sits on His throne.

There is nothing as big as this—the great God in me, living in me now!

No wonder Paul proclaimed, *"I can do all things through Christ which strengtheneth me"* (Philippians 4:13). I am ready for anything because His ability is *mine*. I live in the consciousness of His indwelling presence.

PART II
KEYS TO THE MIRACULOUS

23

CHRISTIANITY IS A MIRACLE

E. W. Kenyon

All religions claim supernatural origins. Christianity not only claims a supernatural origin but also is maintained by the same supernatural power that brought it into being.

THE MIRACLE OF THE BIBLE

The Bible is a miracle book. To those who love it, it is a spring of life and source of power. It is a living message to its own people. It may appear to be dry and dead to those outside the faith, but it is a supernatural book. There is no other book in its class. This one has God in its pages.

> *The word of God is quick, and powerful, and sharper than any twoedged sword, piercing even to the dividing asunder of soul and spirit, and of the joints and marrow, and is a discerner of the thoughts and intents of the heart. Neither is there any creature that is not manifest in his sight.*
> (Hebrews 4:12–13)

In other words, to the believer, the Bible is the living Son of God in print. Yes, the Bible is a miracle.

THE MIRACLE OF THE ISRAELITES

Abraham is our spiritual father. He was a miracle character. His descendants, the Israelites, were a miracle people. They were protected and sustained by miracles.

They saw the Red Sea opened as four million people escaped from Egypt on dry ground. (See Exodus 14.)

They saw a miraculous stream in a desert with enough fresh water to supply all four million people and their herds. (See Exodus 17:1–5.)

They wandered in the wilderness for forty years without any means of support, yet they were fed each morning with manna from heaven. (See Exodus 16.)

Their clothes and sandals never wore out. (See Deuteronomy 29:5.)

A cloud led them during the daytime, and a column of fire led them at night. (See Exodus 13:21.)

They saw the Jordan River obey the voice of Joshua as a servant obeys the voice of his master. (See Joshua 3:14–17.) They saw the walls of great cities fall flat at the word of that same man. (See Joshua 6.)

This is the background of Christianity.

THE LIVING GOD

Jesus was supernaturally conceived. His public ministry was a series of miracles, culminating in His very resurrection from the dead.

Likewise, the birth of the church was also a miracle, and miracles played a vital role in the early church's history. They were so interwoven into its story that one cannot separate the two. When you take the miracles out of Christianity, all you have left is religion.

Christianity is a living thing.

Just as young David said when he stood before the menacing Goliath,

> *Thou comest to me with a sword, and with a spear, and with a shield: but I come to thee in the name of the* Lord *of hosts, the God of the armies of Israel, whom thou hast defied.*
>
> (1 Samuel 17:45)

The Philistine gods of Goliath were dead. David's God was a living God, a miracle-working God. David's young heart reveled with joy that he could be used by the living God of Israel to deliver his people.

Take the miracles out of the history of Israel, and there is nothing left. God was the center around which everything moved.

The same is true with Christianity. Every person, in order to become a Christian, must be "born of God." This is a miracle act. God imparts to us His love, His very nature. We become, by nature, children of God. The impartation of this life is a miracle.

Every answered prayer is a miracle; every victory over sin is a miracle. Every time we influence a person to walk with God and to recognize the lordship of Jesus, it is a miracle act. That God watches over us, cares for us, and fulfills His promises to us is miraculous. The joy that fills our hearts in the midst of trials and tests is a miracle.

All of Christianity is a miracle.

God dwelling in these bodies of ours, making them His home, is a transcendent miracle. God taking possession of our minds, so that He may think His thoughts through us and speak His words through us, is a miracle. The presence of the Holy Spirit during our services of worship is a miracle.

Take away Christianity's spiritual power, and you have nothing left but a system of ethics with demands that cannot be met. But let the miracle elements come in, and God becomes a real presence in our midst. Christianity becomes a living force among the nations of the earth.

If the days of miracles are in the past, the days of Jesus Christ's life in the church are also in the past. If miracles are no more, then the things that make Christianity a living religion are gone. If the days of miracles have passed, God's promises exist only to mock us. Likewise, the statements that Jesus made about His name and the power invested in it also mock us. His name becomes but a dry cloud to a desert land that is crying out for water.

Jesus Christ the same yesterday, and to day, and for ever.
(Hebrews 13:8)

Jesus's name has not lost its power!

God does live!

Christianity is a miracle, the work of a miracle-working God. Don't let anyone deceive you by telling you that the days of miracles have passed. If the days of miracles have passed, then God is no longer God, Christ is no longer Christ, and the Bible is no longer the Word of God.

As long as they are, miracles will be.

24

EXPECT A MIRACLE EVERY DAY

Don Gossett

Here are nine reasons why you can expect God to work miracles in your life:

1. *"Jesus said to him, 'If you can believe, all things are possible to him who believes'"* (Mark 9:23 NKJV).

2. *"I say to you, he who believes in Me, the works that I do he will do also; and greater works than these he will do, because I go to My Father"* (John 14:12 NKJV).

3. *"Whatever you ask in My name, that I will do, that the Father may be glorified in the Son"* (John 14:13 NKJV).

4. *"If you ask anything in My name, I will do it"* (John 14:14 NKJV).

5. *"Now unto him that is able to do exceeding abundantly above all that we ask or think, according to the power that worketh in us"* (Ephesians 3:20).

6. *"If ye have faith as a grain of mustard seed,...nothing shall be impossible unto you"* (Matthew 17:20).

7. *"If two of you shall agree on earth as touching any thing that they shall ask, it shall be done for them of my Father which is in heaven"* (Matthew 18:19).

8. *"God has appointed these in the church: first apostles, second prophets, third teachers, after that miracles, then gifts of healings, helps, administrations, varieties of tongues"* (1 Corinthians 12:28 NKJV).

9. *"To one is given the word of wisdom through the Spirit, to another the word of knowledge through the same Spirit, to another faith by the same Spirit, to another gifts of healings by the same Spirit, to another the working of miracles, to another prophecy, to another discerning of spirits, to another different kinds of tongues, to another the interpretation of tongues"* (1 Corinthians 12:8–10 NKJV).

As you act upon these Scriptures, you can expect the Holy Spirit to minister miracles of healing, financial supply, intervention, deliverance, and salvation of souls. The Lord is ministering these truths to your heart *"that He might make you know that man shall not live by bread alone; but man lives by every word that proceeds from the mouth of the LORD"* (Deuteronomy 8:3).

25

THE MILITANT USE OF THE NAME OF JESUS

Don Gossett

Recently, the Holy Spirit caused me to recall one of the key factors in many of the mighty miracles I have witnessed over the years: the militant use of the name of Jesus!

I, Don Gossett, am nothing by myself. But, clothed in the power and authority of the name of Jesus, I have been used by God to see phenomenal miracles performed! Here are a couple of examples of how the name of Jesus will prevail in spiritual warfare, resulting in miraculous signs and wonders.

MRS. BRYANT

Mrs. Bryant was dying of cancer. She had been carried into one of my prayer services, and, during the singing, I felt compelled to stop the service and minister to her. I boldly cursed the cancer in the powerful name of Jesus. In a matter of minutes, Mrs. Bryant was taken to the restroom by two ladies who assisted her. Right there in that bathroom, the ugly cancer passed out of her body!

HELEN

Helen had been bedridden for many years with a severe heart condition. When she was brought into one of our services, I militantly employed the name of Jesus, commanding her heart to receive healing. Thank God, Helen was raised up and restored to full health for many years!

I have ministered to thousands of people who received instant healing miracles as I spoke the name of Jesus with the anointing of the Holy Spirit. There are others who returned or wrote me a letter to say that God had begun a healing, restoring work for them as I prayed over them.

WHAT IS THE MILITANT USE OF THE NAME OF JESUS?

We have the right, the authority, and the power—given to all children of God by our heavenly Father and manifested through the Holy Spirit—to boldly speak the name of Jesus as a powerful weapon against the enemy.

> *...Whatsoever ye shall ask of the Father in my name, he may give it you.* (John 15:16)

> *And fixing his eyes on [a lame beggar], with John, Peter said, "Look at us." So he gave them his attention, expecting to receive something from them. Then Peter said, "Silver and gold I do not have, but what I do have I give you: In the name of Jesus Christ of Nazareth, rise up and walk." And he took him by the right hand and lifted him up, and immediately his feet and ankle bones received strength. So he, leaping up, stood and walked and entered the temple with them; walking, leaping, and praising God.* (Acts 3:4–8 NKJV)

> *Nor is there salvation in any other, for there is no other name under heaven given among men by which we must be saved.*
> (Acts 4:12 NKJV)

> *Wherefore God also hath highly exalted [Christ Jesus], and given him a name which is above every name.*
> (Philippians 2:9)

The militant use of Jesus's name is the key to activating the miracles you need in your life. God the Father has decreed that this name is supreme above all other names. I have known and practiced this prayer principle for many years, with amazing results for God's glory.

26

IS IT WRONG?

E. W. Kenyon

Making the word of God of none effect…. (Mark 7:13)

Do we not make the Word of God *"of none effect"* by failing to enter into our privileges?

> *That ye may know…what is the exceeding greatness of his power to us-ward who believe, according to the working of his mighty power, which he wrought in Christ….*
> (Ephesians 1:18–20)

Is it not true that God *"wrought in Christ"* an answer to every need and demand of the believer's life? Is it not true that redemption covers absolutely every need of mankind?

For that reason, it is wrong for us to live in spiritual weakness when there is grace to meet every need. Far too many believers have unconsciously put a premium on weakness. We have talked about our unbelief, doubts, and fears as though they were honorary degrees in the spiritual life. We have dignified doubt until, in many places, it is worshipped.

IS IT WRONG TO REMAIN WEAK?

Because we are sons and daughters of God almighty, partakers of His divine nature, it would seem as though it were wrong for us to confess our weaknesses and failures.

> *The LORD is my light and my salvation; whom shall I fear? The LORD is the strength of my life; of whom shall I be afraid?*
> (Psalm 27:1)

If God is the strength of my life, if He comes into my life and imparts Himself to me, then I have the strength of God.

> *Ye are of God, little children, and have overcome them: because greater is he that is in you, than he that is in the world.*
> (1 John 4:4)

"Ye are of God." You came out from God; He is a part of you. He has imparted His own nature to you. Not only that, but He has actually come into your body and now lives within you. He has the same power today that He had when He raised Jesus from the dead. The believer has a right to His strength and ability.

> *God is our refuge and strength, a very present help in trouble.* (Psalm 46:1)

God is the strength of my life, and He is with me now. His life is my life; His strength is my strength. No wonder the apostle Paul said, by the Spirit, *"I can do all things through Christ which strengtheneth me"* (Philippians 4:13).

There is limitlessness about this. This does not mean only physical strength; it also means the ability to meet any kind of need. When Jesus said, *"Ye shall receive power"* (Acts 1:8), He meant, "Ye shall receive ability." The ability of God is given to you.

> *That he would grant you…to be strengthened with might by his Spirit in the inner man.* (Ephesians 3:16)

If your *"inner man"* is made strong, the outer man will respond to that strength. The strength of God for the inner man is the strength of God for the physical man.

IS IT WRONG TO REMAIN EMPTY?

What we mean by "empty" is *unusable*, like a leaky vessel. It is wrong for us, because of who we are in Christ, to be empty and unusable.

> *Giving thanks unto the Father, which hath made us meet to be partakers of the inheritance of the saints in light.* (Colossians 1:12)

We have the ability—the God-given ability—to enjoy the very fullness of our privileges in Christ.

> *And ye are complete in him, which is the head of all principality and power.* (Colossians 2:10)

Your relationship through the "new birth" has brought you into absolute union with God.

> *Therefore if any man be in Christ, he is a new creature.* (2 Corinthians 5:17)

That *"new creature"* is made out of God. It is God's nature, God's life, imparted to your spirit. *"For we are his workmanship, created in Christ Jesus"* (Ephesians 2:10). We are actually members of the body of Christ, physically and spiritually. *"Know ye not that your bodies are the members of Christ?"* (1 Corinthians 6:15). Then, in verse 19, it says, "*Know ye not that your body is the temple of the Holy Ghost which is in you?*"

In the face of this, it is absolutely wrong for us to be found weak and useless when needed.

> *These things have I spoken unto you, that my joy might remain in you, and that your joy might be full.* (John 15:11)

God has planned that you should be filled with joy. That is triumph; that is victory.

In Acts, Scripture says that the disciples *"were all filled with the Holy Spirit"* (Acts 4:31 NKJV). God planned that you should be filled with the Holy Spirit, and that the Spirit's ability should dominate your life. In the presence of grace and ability like this, it is wrong to be empty or weak when you can be filled with all the fullness of God.

IS IT WRONG TO REMAIN ILL?

Sickness and disease came from the fall. In other words, they are the byproducts of satanic dominion over man. Any redemptive act of God that would redeem us from Satan must also redeem us from sickness and disease. Any redemptive act that fails to redeem us from sickness and disease is a limited redemption.

> *But he was wounded for our transgressions, he was bruised for our iniquities: the chastisement of our peace was upon him; and with his stripes we are healed.* (Isaiah 53:5)

Here is redemption by substitution. As God dealt with the sin problem, He also dealt with the disease problem: "*And the* LORD *hath laid on him the iniquity of us all*" (verse 6). Then, verse 10: "*Yet it pleased the* LORD *to bruise him.*" Then, back to verse 4: "*Surely he hath borne our griefs, and carried our sorrows.*" A more literal translation of this verse would be: "He carried our diseases."

In the face of this, it is wrong to remain sick. If God laid our sin on Jesus Christ, it would be wrong for us to live in sin. In the same way, if God laid our diseases on Him, it would be wrong for us to live under the continual dominion of our diseases.

Jesus was the manifest will of the Father. He spent three-fourths of His public ministry healing the sick. He gave the church the use of His name and declared that, in His name, we *"shall lay hands on the sick, and they shall recover"* (Mark 16:18).

> *Is anyone sick among you? let him call for the elders of the church; and let them pray over him, anointing him with oil in the name of the Lord: and the prayer of faith shall save the sick, and the Lord shall raise him up.* (James 5:14–15)

"The Spirit of Him who raised Jesus from the dead dwells in you" (Romans 8:11 NKJV). That same Spirit will heal these mortal bodies of ours. Healing is a part of the plan of redemption.

IS IT WRONG TO REMAIN IN NEED?

It is wrong for me to need clothing, food, and shelter, and not to have them, because I am in God's family. God is my Father, and I am His child.

> *For your heavenly Father knoweth that ye have need of all these things.* (Matthew 6:32)

Here, Scripture is speaking of clothing, food, and the other necessities of life. It says that if we seek first the kingdom of God and His righteousness, He will add all these things unto us. (See verse 33.)

Is this the Word of God? If it is, then I can depend upon it absolutely. If it is just some of the notions of Matthew, John, and Peter, that would be another proposition.

> *My God shall supply all your need according to his riches in glory by Christ Jesus.* (Philippians 4:19)

Here, by *"all your need,"* Paul was referring to food, clothing, and all the physical necessities of life. He declared that the Father God will supply every need of yours. The word *"supply"* means "to make full...to cause to abound, to furnish or supply liberally." Therefore, *"all your need"* means exactly what it says.

In Matthew, we are given a glimpse of the moment before Jesus fed the multitude. He took those five loaves and two fishes and asked the Father's blessing upon them, causing them to multiply. Then, He *"gave the loaves to his disciples, and the disciples to the multitude"* (Matthew 14:19). They had said it could not be done, but He proved to them that it could be done and gave them the bread to give to the multitude. Jesus would not have given us this illustration of His power and grace unless He intended for us to follow in His footsteps.

All of Scripture tells us that Jesus is our example as a healer, feeder, and supplier of the people.

> *Verily, verily, I say unto you, Whatsoever ye shall ask the Father in my name, he will give it you.* (John 16:23)

Jesus has given to the church the "power of attorney" to use His name, the name that has all authority in heaven and on earth. (See Matthew 28:18.) It was the Man who bore that name who performed the miracles. Now, in His name, we can do the same.

IS IT WRONG TO REMAIN IN BONDAGE?

If God has redeemed us at the tremendous cost of His Son's incarnation, His suffering on the cross, His horrifying trip to hades, His triumphant resurrection, and His glorious entrance into the presence of the Father as victor over death and hell, it is a crime for us to remain in bondage.

> *If the Son therefore shall make you free, ye shall be free indeed.* (John 8:36)

The Son has made us free. God declares that we are free. Our unbelief cannot make Him a liar. Our ignorance of our rights and privileges cannot annul the Word or make it of no effect. God says we are free.

> *In* [Christ] *we have redemption through his blood, the forgiveness of sins, according to the riches of his grace.* (Ephesians 1:7)

Again, God declares that we are redeemed, which means that Satan's dominion over us has been broken. Dare to make your confession as strong as this statement:

> [God] *hath delivered us from the power of darkness, and hath translated us into the kingdom of his dear Son: in whom we have redemption....* (Colossians 1:13–14)

This is a description of our redemption. Not only did God break Satan's dominion and power; He also translated us, by the new birth, out of Satan's authority and family and into the kingdom of the Son of His love, and into His own family. That makes you absolutely free in Christ. Satan has no more right to reign over you than he has to reign over Jesus, your Lord and Head. If Satan were able to reign over you, it would prove that God and Jesus are not able to prevent it. The apostle Paul wrote, *"For sin shall not have dominion over you"* (Romans 6:14). A more literal translation would be: "Sin shall not lord it over you." Here, *"sin"* means Satan—Satan shall not lord it over you. If he could lord it over you, and the Father couldn't help it, then Satan would be stronger than God.

But that is not the case.

IS IT WRONG TO REMAIN LOVELESS?

Christianity is really a revelation of love. It is not a system of doctrines, creeds, and laws but a love affair. It is God coming into the human form and living His love life.

> *These things have I written unto you that believe on the name of the Son of God; that ye may know that ye have eternal life, and that ye may believe on the name of the Son of God.*
> (1 John 5:13)

Eternal life is the nature, the substance, and the being of God.

> *Beloved, let us love one another: for love is of God; and every one that loveth is born of God, and knoweth God. He that loveth not knoweth not God; for God is love.* (1 John 4:7–8)

The proof of our having been born from above is that we are lovers, and if any man or woman is not a lover in this sense, he or she is not born of God. A man or woman may be orthodox and subscribe to the creed of the church, may take Communion, and may have been baptized or confirmed, but if he or she is not ruled and dominated by love, he or she is not born again.

This is a severe test, but this is the Father's own statement:

> *We know that we have passed from death unto life, because we love the brethren. He that loveth not his brother abideth in death. Whosoever hateth his brother is a murderer: and ye know that no murderer hath eternal life abiding in him.*
> (1 John 3:14–15)

Death—or the Adamic nature—is union with Satan. The man or woman who does not love has never passed out of death and into life. These verses should be written in capital letters so that everyone who professes the name of Christ might read it. Love is the test and the proof of our union with God.

And we have known and believed the love that God hath to us. God is love; and he that dwelleth in love dwelleth in God, and God in him. (1 John 4:16)

27

THE BOLDER YOUR FAITH

Don Gossett

The lady lay dying. Doctors in two clinics had given the same verdict: she was incurably dying of cancer.

Her husband loved his wife very much and was determined to do everything he could to help her. He brought her need to the attention of a listener of one of our radio broadcasts. This listening friend had heard me challenge believers to take their rights in Christ by daring to lay hands on the sick. My listener friend accepted the challenge of this dying woman's need. His first impulse was to call our ministry to ask for the prayers of those who were used of God to pray for the sick.

Then, he remembered: *"The righteous are bold as a lion"* (Proverbs 28:1). This man knew he was righteous through Christ. Therefore, he became as bold as a lion!

When he was brought before this woman, who was carried in by her husband, he boldly rebuked the foul cancers in the name of Jesus. As he ministered, every demon of hell seemed to attack and tried to cause him to doubt this deliverance. Again, he remembered some words I had spoken: "The bolder your faith, the greater your victory. The bolder your faith, the greater your success."

Unwaveringly, he stood his ground as a devil-defeating master. He was acting on these words of Jesus: *"In my name shall they cast out devils"* (Mark 16:17).

"In the name of Jesus," he said with a voice of authority, "I command you demons of cancer to depart from this woman's body. She is God's child, and you have no right to take her life."

He stood fast to his bold commands in Jesus's name, and the Holy Spirit honored the Word spoken and acted on. The cancer passed from her body, the natural color of her skin returned, and her appetite became normal again. She was restored to full health! This was all confirmed by the same doctors who had previously stated that all was hopeless.

Are you a born-again believer? Do you know that you are righteous? Are you aware that the righteous are as bold as lions? Then, just as this man ministered deliverance to the woman with cancer, you can do the same. Regardless of your name, your age, or your education, you can be the vessel through whom the Lord performs His miraculous works today!

28

COME BOLDLY UNTO THE THRONE OF GRACE

E. W. Kenyon

> *Let us therefore come boldly unto the throne of grace, that we may obtain mercy, and find grace to help in time of need.*
> (Hebrews 4:16)

We come in the name of Jesus. We come on the authority of His own promises, such as: *"Whatsoever ye shall ask in my name, that will I do"* (John 14:13). That word is His word. It makes Him utter the same prayer that our lips are saying.

Or, *"If two of you shall agree on earth as touching any thing that they shall ask, it shall be done for them of my Father which is in heaven"* (Matthew 18:19). When I quote His word, that same word goes before the Father. It is His word, not my word. It is His prayer, not my prayer.

Remember, Jesus also said, *"If ye abide in me, and my words abide in you, ye shall ask what ye will, and it shall be done unto you"* (John 15:7).

I am using Jesus's words. The Father hears the words of Jesus coming from lips yielded to the lordship of His Son, so it is as if His Son is praying through my lips. I remind Him that the Word abides in me and that I abide in Him. There is no ignoring it. It is the Master Himself doing the work. He prays through me.

Before the Father, I say, *"Whatsoever ye shall ask in my name, that will I do, that the Father may be glorified in the Son"* (John 14:13). I say, "I desire that You be glorified through Jesus, so, I am asking in Jesus's name that this thing be done."

Here, the word *"ask"* means "demand." I am demanding that the soreness leave this person's body. I know, by this taking place, that the Father will be glorified. I am taking Jesus's side of the issue and doing the thing that will glorify the Father. When we take this attitude, prayer becomes a God-sized affair. We enter into the fullness of Christ in our prayer life.

Sitting here in my study, I can touch China and the utmost islands of the sea. I can send angel forces to minister to those in need. God's Word becomes the coin of the kingdom. Jesus's name on my lips becomes as though the Master Himself were present. Let us enter into this practice in all its fullness.

29

THE SUPERNATURAL

E. W. Kenyon

Supernatural. The very word smells of miracles. Christianity itself is supernatural. It is the union of deity and humanity. This union was first manifested in the Man from Galilee, and then, again, on the day of Pentecost, when one hundred and twenty men and women were united with deity.

The new birth is a miracle; it is supernatural. It is a partaking of the nature of God. Every child of God is a miracle. When the Spirit comes into a man's body and makes it His home, a miracle has taken place. That person is now capable of living in the Spirit realm, where Jesus lived while He was on earth.

The faith realm, the love realm, and the Spirit realm all represent the plain on which we meet with God. The man who walks by faith and not by reason or feelings is walking in the supernatural. The man who walks in love and who lives in the realm above reason is also supernatural.

Natural man is selfish. The Jesus kind of love takes us out of the realm of selfishness and into the realm of God. The man who walks in the Spirit is walking in the realm above reason and physical evidences. Those things of the world may touch him, but he is not in their realm.

> *Fear thou not; for I am with thee: be not dismayed; for I am thy God: I will strengthen thee; yea, I will help thee; yea, I will uphold thee with the right hand of my righteousness.*
>
> (Isaiah 41:10)

Here is God, actually participating in our daily activities. He is a partner with us in all that we are and all that we do. He is making Himself one with us. His strength becomes our strength. His life is our life. His wisdom, love, and quietness all become ours, as well. We are utterly identified with Him. He becomes a part of every aspect of our lives, and we can say, *"I can do all things through Christ which strengtheneth me"* (Philippians 4:13). It takes us out of the realm of weakness and fear and inability, and into the realm of His own ability.

We become supermen and superwomen. By His grace, we know that *"greater is he that is in you, than he that is in the world"* (1 John 4:4).

Then, we fearlessly take on the impossible. We are not reckoning our weaknesses, limitations, lack of knowledge, or lack of finances; rather, we are reckoning Him who has called us into fellowship with His Son Jesus Christ.

In Him, we are more than conquerors. (See Romans 8:37.)

30

WHAT IS A MIRACLE?

E. W. Kenyon

I once asked a class if they could define a miracle. I shall never forget the looks on the faces of those young men and women. I asked, "Isn't a miracle simply Christ revealing the creative energy of God by acting in the physical realm?"

To my mind, a miracle is God intruding into the sense realm. It is spiritual forces dominating physical forces. When God heals a person, He is making normal what the adversary had distorted. A miracle, therefore, is God restoring what Satan has destroyed.

Jesus was a miracle. His incarnation was miraculous. The senses cannot understand it. It belongs to the spiritual realm. His miracles were all beyond human reasoning. He healed the leper and made pure and wholesome his diseased flesh. He raised from the dead a man who had been in the grave for four days. A man whose body had begun to decay was made completely whole.

He spoke, and the fish of the sea obeyed Him. He commanded a storm to cease, and the water became calm and peaceful. He walked upon the very waves of the sea.

How was He able to do such things? He was God incarnate.

Are miracles a part of the plan of God for us today? The church began with miracles. The new creation is, without a doubt, the master miracle.

Healing the sick is miraculous. Walking on the sea is miraculous. But when God imparted His nature to a man like Saul of Tarsus—a participant in the murders and imprisonment of many men and women of God—in a single moment, that man was made a new creation. That is a miracle, indeed.

Creating a universe is a miracle. But recreating a child of the devil and making him a child of God, imparting to him His own love nature, is, to me, the crowning miracle of all.

When you take the miraculous out of Christianity, you have nothing left but philosophy, and philosophy has never benefitted any heathen nation. It did not make the Greeks any different from the nations that surrounded them, except that they had a higher type of sense-knowledge civilization.

Philosophy never gave to them a scientist, an inventor, a great philanthropist, or a home for orphans and the aged. It did not give the woman any standing. She was bought and sold. They practiced polygamy.

There was nothing that we would exchange our Christian faith for today.

Christianity is a miracle. It is God's intrusion into the human realm.

31

EXPECT GREAT MIRACLES

Don Gossett

Years ago, R. A. Torrey said, "Pray for great things, expect great things, work for great things, but, above all, pray."

One of the most heart-touching stories from my years in the mission field was told to me in Trivandrum, India. The organizer and advance manager of our crusades, V. A. Joseph, shared with me the details.

Mr. DeSousa had a son who had been born blind in both eyes. When he heard about the miraculous answers to prayer taking place at our meetings in the Police Stadium in Trivandrum, it ignited within his heart a spark of faith in the possibility that his son would receive his sight. There was only one problem: the DeSousa home was thirty-five kilometers (around twenty-one miles) from Trivandrum, and Mr. DeSousa didn't have enough money to pay for his son and himself to travel there. Yet the possibility of his son receiving his sight was so compelling, he decided he would take the boy by the hand and walk to the crusade.

This father and son walking side by side must have been an incredible sight. Together, they walked into the Police Stadium. At the climax of each service, I would end with a mass prayer for the healing of all manner of afflictions. For the DeSousas, this would be a night of nights. When I spoke the name of the Lord Jesus for all of those who were blind in one or both eyes, a creative miracle was performed, and the boy's blind eyes were opened.

In that crowd of thousands, only those directly around the DeSousas knew of the immediate impact of what had happened. Later, the boy was met by the examining committee, which consisted of doctors and other medical professionals. They verified that the blind boy had received sight in both of his eyes.

Joyfully, Mr. DeSousa and his son walked all the way back home. No longer was it necessary for the father to lead his son by the hand. Praise the Lord, the boy had perfect sight in a new world of vision and blessing.

> O give thanks unto the LORD; call upon his name: make known his deeds among the people. Sing unto him, sing psalms unto him: talk ye of all his wondrous works....Remember his marvellous works that he hath done. (Psalm 105:1–2, 5)

32

MIRACLE-MINDED

E. W. Kenyon

The world has become "doubt-minded." In the higher realms of education, it is a mark of scholarship to put a question mark after every sentence and to challenge all of the old landmarks.

Doubt is an unhealthy mental condition because questions are a sign of weakness. Doubt has never been a sign of strength. It isn't *doubting* something but *believing* something that makes us strong. Doubts always result in unhealthy reactions; faith always results in healthy reactions.

Blessed is the man who becomes faith-minded toward God, who becomes faith-minded toward the Bible, and who reaches the place where doubt is unwanted, where he shrinks from it with fear. When he has come to the place where faith is cultivated, nurtured, and welcomed, the next step is to become "miracle-minded."

Jesus was miracle-minded. Elijah was miracle-minded. Paul and Peter were both miracle-minded. Once a person, or a group of people, becomes miracle-minded, you will then witness scenes that were common to the first-century church. But among doubt-minded and world-minded people, you will find nothing happening that is out of the ordinary.

Faith-mindedness and miracle-mindedness come from a close walk with the Lord Jesus. I question if anyone can walk closely with the Lord, obeying His Word and submitting to His lordship, without being miracle-minded.

You see, the farther we are from the Master, the dimmer our faith becomes. The nearer we come to Him, the more clearly we see Him through the eyes of faith.

If you are in the place where doubts dominate, you are a long way from the Master.

If you are in the place where faith dominates, you are walking closely to Him.

Unbelief, then, might also be called "distance."

Faith might also be called "nearness."

Miracle-mindedness makes prayer a business proposition. You are investing time and thought into your prayer life and drawing dividends as a result. You are seeing God work.

Many Christians remain faith-minded. As a result, every week, we see staggering miracles performed. We see miracles that our scientific friends say are impossible. And we agree with them.

33

TURNING WATER INTO WINE

Don Gossett

The third day there was a marriage in Cana of Galilee; and the mother of Jesus was there: and both Jesus was called, and his disciples, to the marriage. And when they wanted wine, the mother of Jesus saith unto him, They have no wine. Jesus saith unto her, Woman, what have I to do with thee? mine hour is not yet come. His mother saith unto the servants, Whatsoever he saith unto you, do it. And there were set there six waterpots of stone, after the manner of the purifying of the Jews, containing two or three firkins apiece. Jesus saith unto them, Fill the waterpots with water. And they filled them up to the brim. And he saith unto them, Draw out now, and bear unto the governor of the feast. And they bare it. When the ruler of the feast had tasted the water that was made wine, and knew not whence it was: (but the servants which drew the water knew;) the governor of the feast called the bridegroom, and saith unto him, Every man at the beginning doth set forth good wine; and when men have well drunk, then that which is worse: but thou

> *hast kept the good wine until now. This beginning of miracles did Jesus in Cana of Galilee, and manifested forth his glory; and his disciples believed on him.* (John 2:1–11)

Jesus turned the water into wine! He spoke the miracle into existence with these words: *"Fill the waterpots with water."* His words were spirit and life. (See John 6:63.) He spoke words that worked wonders! This creative miracle of Jesus's is being duplicated in our modem day by other creative miracles that bring glory to God and deliverance to people.

A NEW KNEECAP FOR A MAN NAMED "LUCKY"

I once went to a city in Oregon for a salvation and healing crusade. There, the Lord was *"working with them, and confirming the word with signs following"* (Mark 16:20). One night, a man named Lucky Metz walked to the front of the auditorium. He had a pronounced limp, and when I asked him what he wanted prayer for, he explained that he had suffered an accident twenty-two years ago that had damaged his knee, requiring surgery to remove the entire kneecap.

I said, "Though your name is Lucky, you haven't been very lucky, have you? Before I pray for you, I want to ask you, have you received Jesus as your Savior?"

When he replied that he had not, I shared the good news of the gospel with him.

"Lucky," I said, "you can go to heaven without a kneecap, but you can never enter heaven unless you are born again. More important than the possibility of your receiving a new kneecap as we pray for you tonight, you need to open your heart and confess Jesus as your Lord and Savior."

Without hesitation, Lucky prayed the sinner's prayer with me and became a saved man. Praise the Lord! Then, I spoke these words: "Lord Jesus, when You walked here on earth, You performed a creative miracle by turning water into wine at Cana. In Your name, Lord, I speak for a new kneecap to be created for Lucky right now."

Amazingly, when he rolled up the leg of his pants, Lucky discovered that the Lord had done just as I had asked Him to. Lucky Metz had a new kneecap! He circled the church auditorium, walking without the heavy limp. He was beside himself with delight! Our Creator God had performed for this man an awesome miracle—a new kneecap.

Lucky returned to the church for the next service, praising God for His saving grace and His creative healing power. Though he'd been quite unlucky for the previous twenty-two years, by grace, he had received two wondrous gifts: salvation and a new kneecap!

His physician, a Dr. Thomas, had X-rays in his office proving that Lucky had had no kneecap for those many years. After the Lord had performed this miracle, this physician shared his reaction: "Only twice before in my many years of practice have I seen such an instantaneous miracle. This was indeed the work of a greater Physician."

I repeat the statement of Dr. Thomas: "This was indeed the work of a greater Physician." His name is Jesus, *"who went about doing good, and healing all that were oppressed of the devil; for God was with him"* (Acts 10:38).

The Lord used me to speak a new kneecap into existence for this man. Yet nothing happened until I spoke in Jesus's name for this wonder of God!

You, too, can speak miracles into existence by speaking with the authority of Jesus Christ. Be bold in your believing and speaking. *"I believed, and therefore have I spoken"* (2 Corinthians 4:13).

34

LORD, GIVE US BILLS TO PAY

Don Gossett

Family prayer has always been a highlight of our home. When my children were young, witnessing their simple faith in God was an inspiration to me, especially how they expressed their love for the Lord in singing, reciting Bible verses, and praying. These were lessons for us adults, who often become so formal in spiritual matters.

One evening, when my daughter Judy was four years old, we had a family prayer time I'll never forget. Judy had overheard my wife and me discussing some crucial financial matters. Unfortunately, she had heard us blame each other for the bills that had gone unpaid. The phrase "unpaid bills" seemed to resonate in Judy's little mind. Our procedure in family prayer was to sit in a circle and allow our five children to take turns praying. When it was Judy's turn, she prayed, "Lord, give us strong food to eat; and, Lord, give us strong clothes to wear; and, dear Lord, give us bills to pay."

I was amazed for a moment by her prayer. It was amusing but deeply earnest from her little heart. Also, I was quite sure the "dear Lord" understood her petition even better than I.

After our prayer time, I called for Judy to come to me. I hugged her and said, "Judy, I know the Lord heard your prayer and knows all about it. But one thing you never need to ask for is unpaid bills. They are like the devil; they are ever present to harass us."

When we are faced with great financial obligations, I remember Judy's prayer and take courage in the fact that the Lord *does* understand our lack and assures us that He will supply our every need. *"My God shall supply all your need according to his riches in glory by Christ Jesus"* (Philippians 4:19).

God wants to provide for our unpaid bills. God is love. His promises are sure.

35

DON'T SAY "I CAN'T" WHEN GOD SAYS "YOU CAN"

Don Gossett

The phrase "I can't" is nowhere in the Bible. We must begin to speak God's language and proclaim only what His Word says.

DON'T SAY, "I CAN'T RECEIVE MY HEALING."

Boldly say, "I *can* receive my healing, for *'with his stripes* [I am] *healed'* (Isaiah 53:5). I *can* receive my healing because Jesus said, *'They shall lay hands on the sick, and they shall recover'* (Mark 16:18). Hands have been laid on me; thus, I am recovering."

DON'T SAY, "I CAN'T PAY MY BILLS."

Declare emphatically, "I *can* pay my bills, for *'my God shall supply all your need according to his riches in glory by Christ Jesus'* (Philippians 4:19). I have honored the Lord by paying my tithes and giving offerings in His name, and He says He will *'open…the windows of heaven, and pour you out a blessing, that there shall not be room enough to receive it'* (Malachi 3:10). Then, He will *'rebuke the* devourer' (verse 11) for my sake. I *can* pay my bills because my God supplies the money to meet my every need."

DON'T SAY, "I CAN'T WITNESS IN POWER."

Defeat that negative statement by affirming, "I *can* witness in power, for I have received the Holy Spirit into my life. Jesus said, *"You shall receive power when the Holy Spirit has come upon you; and you shall be witnesses to Me"* (Acts 1:8 NKJV). I *can* share my testimony—my witness for Christ, the message of His salvation—with great effectiveness because I am energized by the mighty Holy Spirit from heaven."

DON'T SAY, "I CAN'T RECEIVE ANSWERS TO MY PRAYERS."

This kind of expression will close the heavens to your life. With assurance, speak out, "I *can* receive answers to my prayers, for Jesus said that whatever I ask the Father in His name, the Father will give to me. I *can* receive mighty answers from God, for Jesus has promised, *'If ye shall ask any thing in my name, I will do it'* (John 14:14). If I call on God, He has said, *'I will answer thee, and show thee great and mighty things'* (Jeremiah 33:3). This is my confidence in Him, that whatever I ask from Him, I will receive, because I 'keep his commandments, and do those things that are pleasing in his sight' (1 John 3:22)."

DON'T SAY, "MY LOVED ONES WILL NEVER BE WON TO JESUS CHRIST."

That is a lie of the devil. For you to speak it is to give power to the devil. Agree with God's promise and declare it: "I *can* see my loved ones all won to Jesus Christ, for God has said, *'Believe on the Lord Jesus Christ, and thou shalt be saved, and thy house'* (Acts 16:31). I shall never fear that my loved ones will be lost forever in hell. I *can* see all my loved ones saved because I am God's instrument to believe for their salvation."

DON'T SAY, "I CAN'T OVERCOME MY WEIGHT CONDITION."

Discover the ability of Christ by saying, "'*I can* do all things through Christ which strengtheneth me' (Philippians 4:13). Through Christ, I *can* resist eating rich, fattening foods. Through Christ, I *can* avoid highly caloric foods. I *can*, by God's grace, eat with moderation and temperance, for my belly shall not be my god. I *can* learn to eat nutritiously and healthfully. I *can* conquer my weight condition through Jesus Christ, who is my strength and my sufficiency."

PART III
KEYS TO HEALING

36

KEYS TO A LONG, SATISFYING LIFE

Don Gossett

With long life I will satisfy him, and show him my salvation.
(Psalm 91:16)

My friend Kenneth Hagin used to say, "If, someday, you hear that I'm gone, you'll know that I got satisfied." In his eighty-eighth year, he "got satisfied"!

[The Lord] *satisfieth thy mouth with good things; so that thy youth is renewed like the eagle's.* (Psalm 103:5)

Don't think about how old you are. Think only about what you can accomplish. Then, go and do it! That alone is living.

I once met the great evangelist Reinhard Bonnke at a convention. When he saw my name tag, he exclaimed, "Don Gossett, I've read many of your father's books!" I later told my wife about this exchange and exclaimed, "The Lord must be renewing my youth. Bonnke thought it was my father who wrote these books!"

> *Teach us to number our days, that we may apply our hearts unto wisdom.* (Psalm 90:12)

It was James Farley who declared, "Never think any 'oldish' thoughts. It's 'oldish' thoughts that make a person old. How do you live to be eighty years old? By counting your days, one day at a time!"

> *This one thing I do, forgetting those things which are behind, and reaching forth unto those things which are before....* (Philippians 3:13)

Live your life and forget your age. Your age is just a number. Sharpen your vision. Elevate your goals!

> *What man is he that desireth life, and loveth many days, that he may see good? Keep thy tongue from evil, and thy lips from speaking guile. Depart from evil, and do good; seek peace, and pursue it.* (Psalm 34:12–14)

Dr. John A. Schindler asked, "Look, are you peaceful and happy enough to live a long time?"

> *...but the tongue of the wise is health.* (Proverbs 12:18)

The word *healthy* is defined as "being sound in body, mind, or spirit;...freedom from physical disease or pain." William Danforth wrote the excellent book *I Dare You*. I delight in his exhortation, "I dare you to be healthy, live a long time, and never think old age."

> *A merry heart doeth good like a medicine.* (Proverbs 17:22)

Bernard Baruch attributed his long life to his humorous attitude, saying, "To me, old age is always fifteen years older than I am."

37

THE LIVING WORD

E. W. Kenyon

The words that I speak unto you, they are spirit, and they are life. (John 6:63)

What a ring of certainty there is in every word that drops from the lips of the Master. There are no theories on the lips of Jesus. Every word that He says is a part of Himself. He is truth, and that truth is Jesus in reality. Therefore, every word that departs from His lips is real. His words are God-filled words.

Ages may pass, and yet that word will be as living and as real as the day it was uttered. Time and distance have no effects upon the Word of God.

For the word of God is quick, and powerful.... (Hebrews 4:12)

A more literal translation of this verse would read: "The Word of God is a living thing."

That Word is Christ Himself. I cannot understand how it can be Christ, but I simply know that it is.

Dealing with a "living thing" has a thrill and romance to it. I read God's Word as though it had come to me that morning and had been addressed to no one else. It is my own personal message from my Master, Jesus. It is not only a living thing, but it is also the very food of my spirit nature. It is that Word that God said He would send to heal us. Every word of God is part of God. God is in His Word.

The skeptic cannot see it. It is a root out of dry ground to him. But, to us who believe, that Word throbs with the very life of our Father.

The healing of our physical bodies comes through the Word, which declares that *"with his stripes we are healed"* (Isaiah 53:5). I read that truth over and over again, until it grows into me and becomes a part of me. I meditate on it until it burns within me, until I look up and whisper softly, "This is Thine own message to me. I understand now that, by the stripes that were put upon my Master, Jesus, I am healed."

My heart overflows with praise and worship and love. He has healed me through the living Word. His own Word has spoken to this heart of mine.

38

SOME FACTS ABOUT HEALING

E. W. Kenyon

From a study of Isaiah 53, it is evident that healing is a part of the plan of redemption.

If it is, then, the moment that you accept Christ as your Savior and confess Him as your Lord, you have a right to the virtue that is in that redemption, the healing of your sick body.

Healing belongs to every child of God.

Some say that it is not the will of God to heal everyone. There is no scriptural evidence to that effect, however.

They say, "Didn't Paul have a thorn in the flesh?"

Yes. However, Paul's thorn in the flesh was not an illness but a demon interfering with his speech and causing him to stammer. This "thorn" came upon Paul because of the exceeding greatness of the revelation that had been given to him. None of us can hide behind that excuse because none of us has ever had a revelation like Paul did.

Another skeptic says, "Didn't Jesus heal some while allowing others to remain sick?"

There is no doubt that He did. There was sickness among the disciples, just as there is sickness in the church today, but that is because the early Christians came directly out of heathenism. They knew nothing about the Lord and broke fellowship with Him, as many of us break fellowship with Him today. The adversary attacked them as he attacks us today. If they had fully understood their privileges, they might have known how to maintain their fellowship and their health.

We, however, know that neither Peter nor James nor John ever laid hands upon a person who was not healed. We cannot find a place where the Bible says that it is not the will of God to heal everyone.

I would not argue about it. I would take what belongs to me.

I don't love disease enough, and I don't believe that anyone reading this book loves disease and sickness enough, to argue the question. I believe we would rather get rid of our troubles.

39

THREE TYPES OF HEALING

E. W. Kenyon

It is always pleasant to hear new teachings on an old subject, especially one about which many feel that they know the last word. However, I think we have discovered the reason why many have arrived at a place where they no longer have their prayers for healing answered, while others have received healing many times over.

Remember that in Jesus's teaching, He based healing entirely on the grounds of faith. In almost every case, He demanded faith, but the man beside the pool of Bethesda was healed without any faith on his part. John 5 relates that man's story:

> Now there is at Jerusalem by the sheep market a pool, which is called in the Hebrew tongue Bethesda, having five porches. In these lay a great multitude of impotent folk, of blind, halt, withered, waiting for the moving of the water. For an angel went down at a certain season into the pool, and troubled the water: whosoever then first after the troubling of the water stepped in was made whole of whatsoever disease he had. And

> *a certain man was there, which had an infirmity thirty and eight years. When Jesus saw him lie, and knew that he had been now a long time in that case, he saith unto him, Wilt thou be made whole? The impotent man answered him, Sir, I have no man, when the water is troubled, to put me into the pool: but while I am coming, another steppeth down before me. Jesus saith unto him, Rise, take up thy bed, and walk. And immediately the man was made whole, and took up his bed, and walked.* (verses 2–9)

But one of the most striking examples in the entire ministry of the Master is the case of the centurion, as recorded in Matthew 8:5–13. A centurion came to Jesus, beseeching Him to heal his servant, who was home sick with palsy. Jesus offered to go to his home and heal him, but the centurion answered, "*Speak the word only, and my servant shall be healed*" (verse 8). Jesus turned to the centurion and said, "*Go thy way; and as thou hast believed, so be it done unto thee*" (verse 13). "*And his servant was healed in the selfsame hour*" (verse 13).

In Matthew 9, we find the story of a woman who forced her way through a crowd to touch the hem of Jesus's garment, that she might be made whole. Jesus said to her, "*Daughter, be of good comfort; thy faith hath made thee whole*" (verse 22). In verse 29, Jesus summed up our understanding of healing. He had been followed by two blind men, who cried after Him, saying, "*Thou son of David, have mercy on us*" (verse 27). When He reached His destination, the two men were still there.

> *And Jesus saith unto them, Believe ye that I am able to do this? They said unto him, Yea, Lord. Then touched he their eyes, saying, According to your faith be it unto you.*
> (Matthew 9:28–29)

We must understand that Jesus was dealing with Old Testament people. At this time, no one had been born again. No one knew that Jesus Christ would be their substitute. No one knew that He would be made sin for them. No one knew that He would go to hell for them, to conquer death and the grave. No one knew that He would arise from the dead as their High Priest. No one knew about the new creation.

Thus, you can understand that their faith in Jesus was based purely upon "sense-knowledge faith." This is the type of faith that Thomas had. In the gospel of John, Thomas declared, *"Except I shall see in his hands the print of the nails, and put my finger into the print of the nails, and thrust my hand into his side, I will not believe"* (John 20:25). This is "sense-knowledge faith." Thomas would believe it if he could see it and touch it. Sense-knowledge says, in effect, "I will believe it if I can see it, hear it, feel it, and experience it." Thomas' faith was measured by his senses, not by the Word of God.

Then, Jesus suddenly appeared in the midst of His disciples.

> *Then saith [Jesus] to Thomas, Reach hither thy finger, and behold my hands; and reach hither thy hand, and thrust it into my side: and be not faithless, but believing. And Thomas answered and said unto him, My Lord and my God. Jesus saith unto him, Thomas, because thou hast seen me, thou hast believed: blessed are they that have not seen, and yet have believed.* (John 20:27–29)

"Because thou hast seen me, thou hast believed." That hurts a bit, doesn't it? It hurt the Master even more. There is no unbelief like the unbelief of the senses. *"This is the work of God, that ye believe on him whom he hath sent"* (John 6:29). It is hard for those of us who are familiar with Paul's revelation of what Jesus did for us in the substitutionary sacrifice not to carry it over into the four Gospels.

If we could eliminate all that we know of Christ through the Pauline revelation and see Jesus as those who walked with Him did, we could then appreciate their unbelief. You may wonder,

Didn't Mary believe on Him? Yes, they all believed on Jesus as they lived in close fellowship with Him. But what exactly did they believe?

They did not believe that He was their substitute for sin or that He was going to die for their sins in accordance with Scripture. They did not fully believe in His resurrection, even after they had seen Him resurrected.

What did they believe? They believed that He was a prophet and, in some way, the Son of God. There was evidently no knowledge of Christ having borne our sicknesses and diseases. We do know that what Jesus said to His disciples, as recorded in Mark, was fulfilled, and that God worked with them, *"confirming the word with signs following"* (Mark 16:20).

The disciples' means of advertisement was healing the sick and performing miracles. According to Mark, the unsaved man has a perfect right to healing. One cannot blame the gospel authors for their unbelief. The whole thing was so absolutely new and out of the realm of the senses that you cannot find fault with them.

Now, I want to show you the three types, or classes, of healing.

The first comes by the faith of the sick person, as you have seen in Jesus's teachings. The second comes by the faith of the sick person in the elders' faith. Finally, there is the believer who knows that his diseases and sicknesses were laid upon Jesus. He knows that Jesus put disease and sickness away, and that *"with his stripes [he is] healed."*

> *And they went forth, and preached every where, the Lord working with them, and confirming the word with signs following.* (Mark 16:20)

After the day of Pentecost, the disciples went forth, preaching in the name of Jesus among the heathens and Jews, yet they did not have any conception of the substitutionary sacrifice of their

Master, in whose name they healed the sick and cast out demons. We have a sample of this in the book of Acts:

> And there sat a certain man at Lystra, impotent in his feet, being a cripple from his mother's womb, who never had walked: the same heard Paul speak: who stedfastly beholding him, and perceiving that he had faith to be healed, said with a loud voice, Stand upright on thy feet. And he leaped and walked. (Acts 14:8–10)

Paul did not lay his hands on the man. He did not pray over him. We cannot be certain of what Paul told him, but we do know that he was not a Christian. The man had been listening to the Word, and, as he listened, his heart believed without any doubt. Paul, with the discernment of love, saw it in his eyes, and *"said with a loud voice, Stand upright on thy feet."*

I want you to notice the next group of people who have a right to healing. They are the ones described in 1 Corinthians 3:1: *"And I, brethren, could not speak unto you as unto spiritual, but as unto carnal, even as unto babes in Christ."*

The word *"carnal"* is another way to identify "those ruled by their senses." "Carnal" people are dominated by what they see, hear, feel, smell, and taste. Now, look at the next two verses:

> *I have fed you with milk, and not with meat: for hitherto ye were not able to bear it, neither yet now are ye able. For ye are yet carnal:...are ye not carnal, and walk as men?* (verses 2–3)

In other words, "You walk as sense-ruled men who have never been born again." The Greek word translated as *"carnal"* is *sarkikos*, meaning "sense-ruled" or "senses." The "sense-ruled" man may be born again but is untrained in the Scriptures.

> *For when for the time ye ought to be teachers, ye have need that one teach you again which be the first principles of the oracles*

> *of God; and are become such as have need of milk, and not of strong meat. For every one that useth milk is unskilful in the word of righteousness: for he is a babe.* (Hebrews 5:12–13)

He is but *"a babe."* Or, a better rendering: "He is not experienced in practicing and living in the realm of righteousness."

What does that mean?

Righteousness is the ability to stand in the Father's presence without a sense of condemnation or unworthiness, or in the presence of Satan, disease, and adverse circumstances without fear. It is knowing that, in the name of Jesus, you are a master over demons, disease, and circumstances.

Peter and Paul knew that they were masters in the name of Jesus. They commanded the sick to be healed in that mighty name.

> *But strong meat belongeth to them that are of full age, even those who by reason of use have their senses exercised to discern both good and evil.* (Hebrews 5:14)

Now, let's look at James 5:14–16:

> *Is any sick among you? let him call for the elders of the church; and let them pray over him, anointing him with oil in the name of the Lord: and the prayer of faith shall save the sick, and the Lord shall raise him up; and if he have committed sins, they shall be forgiven him. Confess your faults one to another, and pray one for another, that ye may be healed. The effectual fervent prayer of a righteous man availeth much.*

Notice that, first, the sick one confesses, and then the elders pray for him. The sick one, although a Christian, has never taken advantage of what he is in Christ.

> *Surely he hath borne our griefs, and carried our sorrows: yet we did esteem him stricken, smitten of God, and afflicted. But*

> *he was wounded for our transgressions, he was bruised for our iniquities: the chastisement of our peace was upon him; and with his stripes we are healed.* (Isaiah 53:4–5)

It goes without saying that this Scripture refers to the substitutionary sacrifice of Christ. Here, the Holy Spirit puts physical healing before the sin problem. Why? He knows that because we live in physical bodies, we are sense-ruled people. Because of this, He dealt with the physical bodies first.

Notice that Christians have been healed when their sins have been laid on Christ. Isaiah 53:10 clears this up:

> *Yet it pleased the* L*ord* *to bruise him; he hath put him to grief: when thou shalt make his soul an offering for sin, he shall see his seed, he shall prolong his days, and the pleasure of the* L*ord* *shall prosper in his hand.*

You see, God made Jesus a perfect substitute. Sick folks who do not understand the substitutionary sacrifice are clearly relying on the faith of the elders instead of on what Christ did for them in His substitution.

There are three facts I would like you to notice:

First, the sick Christian often does not recognize his substitutionary rights in Christ. He does not realize that a proper amount of faith is not a prerequisite and that healing belongs to him just as much as Jesus's ministry at the right hand of the Father belongs to him. All he has to do is look up and say, "Father, I thank You for my perfect healing, in Jesus's name."

This sick person may be out of fellowship, allowing the adversary to take advantage of him. He calls for the elders of the church to come, and he confesses his sins to them—or, perhaps, to the Father. He is forgiven the moment the confession is made. The elders pray for him, and it is their faith that heals him.

In his sickness, he has brushed aside the substitutionary work of Christ by asking for the elders' faith to heal him. He does this in ignorance, and grace overlooks it.

How many sick folks are there today who are waiting for somebody to pray the *"prayer of faith"* over them? Isaiah 53 is utterly ignored. The work that Jesus did from the time He was made sin until He sat down at the right hand of the Father is ignored. The sick man can see the elders; he can feel them anointing him with oil; he can hear the prayers of faith. You see, he is living in the realm of the senses. He has the same kind of faith that Thomas had.

He is inexperienced in righteousness. He has never taken his place as a righteous man. He has never done the works of a righteous man. He has never borne the fruits of a righteous man.

A righteous man has a legal standing with the Father. He can approach the Father at any time. The righteous man is always bearing the burdens of others in prayer.

Did you notice that *"the effectual fervent prayer of a righteous man availeth much"* (James 5:16)? The prayer of a righteous man is always heard. He is not afraid of sickness or disease. He is a master in every circumstance.

Who is righteous? Every new creation is "the righteousness of God in Christ."

> He hath made him to be sin for us, who knew no sin; that we might be made the righteousness of God in him.
> (2 Corinthians 5:21)

Now, you can see how the sick man has repudiated the work that the Father did in Christ by requesting that someone pray the prayer of faith for him. He is requesting that someone heal him independently of that work.

You ask, "Do you not pray and anoint the sick?"

Yes, if I cannot instruct them of their rights in Christ. I meet them right where they are, as the Master did.

The third class of healing belongs to the new-creation man who knows his Father, knows his rights and privileges in Christ, and knows that Jesus *"took [his] infirmities, and bare [his] diseases"* (Matthew 8:17). He is taking his healing on the grounds of the substitutionary sacrifice of Christ.

Here are some facts I want you to note:

The believer owns all of the rights that Jesus paid for.

All that Jesus did for him in His substitutionary sacrifice belongs to him.

He has come to act on the Word as he would act on the word of a loved one.

It is not a problem of faith. He has no conscious need of faith.

Why? Because he is healed. God does not need to heal him again. He has been healed.

The believer simply accepts the fact that God's Word cannot be broken. He knows that God said, *"I will hasten my word to perform it"* (Jeremiah 1:12).

No word from God is void of fulfillment.

The disease has touched his body. He demands that Satan, the author of all disease, take the unclean thing away, in the name of Jesus. It does not belong to him, for his Father laid that disease on Jesus.

Then, he looks and says, "Father, I thank You for my perfect deliverance. I thank You that Your Word has proven true again, and that by His stripes, I am healed."

40

CAN GOD HEAL?

E. W. Kenyon

God created man. It was He who designed all the delicate organs of the body—the eye, the ear, the brain, and so on. He had the blueprints for the perfect man before Him, detailing every organ and every nerve, every vein, and every artery. When He spoke man into being, He said, *"Let us make man in our image, after our likeness"* (Genesis 1:26).

Man was created and became God's very child. He could look into the face of the Omnipotent and say, "My Father." He was able to hear the reply coming back, "My child."

You ask me, "Can God heal?" He knows where every organ is in the body; He is the logical healer.

I do not discredit the knowledge of the doctor or surgeon nor the blessing that they have been to the men and women who live in the sense realm, especially people who have no God, who have nothing but the arm of flesh. I thank God for all that surgeons and doctors have done.

As believers, however, we have something better. We are not resting on the arm of flesh. We have come to know God. Men and women, if Jesus Christ could raise Lazarus from the dead when his body was decaying and his flesh had become loose upon his bones, then He can heal the sick today.

Is God able? God is the Creator.

Is He willing? That is a part of His plan of redemption for us. He sent His Son to destroy the work of the devil. One of the awful things that Satan does is to bring sickness and disease into the lives of the sons of men.

Jesus came and healed the sick from the very first days of His ministry to the very last days. Yes, healing is a part of the plan of God. When Israel came out of Egypt, God said,

> *If thou wilt diligently hearken to the voice of the LORD thy God, and wilt do that which is right in his sight, and wilt give ear to his commandments, and keep all his statutes, I will put none of these diseases upon thee, which I have brought upon the Egyptians: for I am the LORD that healeth thee.*
> (Exodus 15:26)

> *He brought them forth also with silver and gold: and there was not one feeble person among their tribes.* (Psalm 105:37)

> *I will take sickness away from the midst of thee. There shall nothing cast their young, nor be barren, in thy land: the number of thy days I will fulfil.* (Exodus 23:25–26)

Notice that God promised to take their sickness away as long as they kept the covenant.

"There shall nothing cast their young." In other words, there were no abortions or stillborn babies. There were no barren wives. No young people died prematurely.

> Bless the LORD, O my soul, and forget not all his benefits: who forgiveth all thine iniquities; who healeth all thy diseases; who redeemeth thy life from destruction; who crowneth thee with lovingkindness and tender mercies; who satisfieth thy mouth with good things; so that thy youth is renewed like the eagle's.
> (Psalm 103:2–5)

This is God's dream. Now you can see that disease and sickness are linked together in Jesus's teaching: after He had healed the sick, Jesus said to them, "*Go, and sin no more*" (John 8:11).

> For thus saith the LORD that created the heavens; God himself that formed the earth and made it; he hath established it, he created it not in vain, he formed it to be inhabited.
> (Isaiah 45:18)

This is the Creator. He created the earth and said, "*Let us make man in our image.*" This is the God who is able to heal. Sin and disease are one, and both were laid upon Christ. He bore them.

In the Gospels, Jesus said, "*Go thy way; thy faith hath made thee **whole***" (Mark 10:52, emphasis added). The Greek word for "*whole*" is *sozo*. Ephesians 2:8 says, "*By grace are ye saved through faith; and that not of yourselves: it is the gift of God.*" Here, the Greek word for "*saved*" is also *sozo*. It is a wonderful thing that the Greek word *sozo* is translated interchangeably in the Scriptures for both healing and salvation.

> If thou shalt confess with thy mouth the Lord Jesus, and shalt believe in thine heart that God hath raised him from the dead, thou shalt be saved.
> (Romans 10:9)

This is healing, or salvation. Healing comes by the confession of the lordship of Jesus Christ.

41

HEALING BEGINS IN YOUR MOUTH

Don Gossett

What do you do when your doctor writes out your death certificate while you are still breathing? Is there any hope when the physician says your life on earth is almost over?

Sten Nilsson, a Swedish missionary to India, related this true story:

> When I was a young boy, I was very ill. I overheard the doctor say to my mother, "You need not call for me to make out Sten's death certificate. I'll write it out now." When I heard that, I declared emphatically, "I do not intend to die. I intend to be a missionary in India!" I quoted Scripture: "Death and life are in the power of the tongue" (Proverbs 18:21). The next morning, I got out of my bed and was soon the picture of health.

The key to releasing Sten's faith was the proclamation that came out of his mouth. In the quest for healing, it is truly helpful if you have a purpose in life to be well. Sten had a purpose, indeed: to be a missionary to India.

Remember, unlimited power is released when you speak life-giving words of faith. No matter what you are going through, there is life-altering power in the utterance of God's Word. When you make bold declarations from God's Word, you are speaking with authority and power. Start speaking now and get ready to experience healing power in your life. When you speak His Word, the Holy Spirit helps you to remain steady and unruffled, even in the face of severe challenge and adversity.

Speaking the Word with confidence will enable you to fulfill God's plan and purpose for your life, just as it did for Sten. The Bible says that it is *"by your words you will be justified, and by your words you will be condemned"* (Matthew 12:37). Guard your lips by speaking His promises over your life and the lives of others.

Start every day by boldly declaring, *"The LORD is the strength of my life"* (Psalm 27:1). Declare that you are healed, healthy, and whole. When you receive a bad report, refuse to be shaken. Choose to believe the Lord's good report.

I admire the testimony of Sten Nilsson. No matter the doctor's report, Sten spoke words of faith that resulted in healing. His faith words prevailed over medical knowledge. He didn't deny the existence of sickness. Instead, he denied sickness's right to bring him to an untimely death.

Your words have power. God spoke the universe into being. (See John 1:1.) Jesus said,

> *For verily I say unto you, that whosoever shall say unto this mountain, Be thou removed, and be thou cast into the sea; and shall not doubt in his heart, but shall believe that those things which he saith shall come to pass; he shall have whatsoever he saith.* (Mark 11:23)

Because Jesus said to do it, and because you are obedient to His commands, speak to the mountains in your life—sickness, lack, family issues—and they shall be overcome. Today's mountain is tomorrow's testimony. It doesn't matter how big the mountain is or how long it has been there. What matters is what Jesus said about the mountain—you can be victorious over the mountains of life if you will only speak up!

Like Sten, who spoke life instead of death, you can be full of vim, vigor, and vitality.

42

NOTHING HAPPENED UNTIL I SPOKE THE WORD

Don Gossett

It came to pass, that, as the people pressed upon him to hear the word of God, he stood by the lake of Gennesaret, and saw two ships standing by the lake: but the fishermen were gone out of them, and were washing their nets. And he entered into one of the ships, which was Simon's, and prayed him that he would thrust out a little from the land. And he sat down, and taught the people out of the ship. Now when he had left speaking, he said unto Simon, Launch out into the deep, and let down your nets for a draught. And Simon answering said unto him, Master, we have toiled all the night, and have taken nothing: nevertheless at thy word I will let down the net. And when they had this done, they enclosed a great multitude of fishes: and their net brake. And they beckoned unto their partners, which were in the other ship, that they should come and help them. And they came, and filled both the ships, so that they began to sink. (Luke 5:1–7)

It was when Jesus spoke, saying, *"Launch out into the deep, and let down your nets for a draught,"* that the miraculous catch of fish became theirs. Nothing happened until Jesus spoke the word.

Many times, I've experienced the impossible becoming reality by the authority of the spoken Word. In those situations, again, nothing happened until I spoke His Word.

REVERSING THE IMPOSSIBLE FOR MY CAR PAYMENT

One of my early experiences with reversing the impossible by the power of the spoken Word had to do with a late car payment. Five days after the due date, a collector from the finance company that held the note to my car was at my front door. Abruptly, he explained my options: I could make the payment immediately, or he could take the car.

I protested, "That can't happen. I must have the car for my travels as an evangelist. Can you give me five more days? I know I will have the money by then."

Without an inkling of concern or sympathy, the man reiterated the original options: I could pay today, or he would come back later in the day to repossess the car. Walking to his vehicle, he yelled something else at me: "By the way, I suggest you clean out your car of personal items. When I come back, I'll have no time to wait for that to be done."

I felt a strong temptation to panic and give up. The principle of speaking God's Word was new to me at the time. I considered cleaning out my car but then said, "I will not do that. My God will supply this urgent need today." I walked up and down the hallway of my home, affirming, "My God shall supply all my need." (See Philippians 4:19.) I continued to repeat it scores of times with faith and fervor. After some time, I "felt" the money in my pocket. That was the feeling of faith. Of course, there was no money there, but, by sheer faith, I felt that I possessed it in advance of actually holding it in my hands.

After an hour or so, it became a song in my heart. "My God shall supply all my need." I laughed, I shouted, I held my heart steady with the sure Word of God. "My God shall supply all my need!"

In the natural, it was impossible. There was no way to secure that much money on such short notice. I had no relatives from whom I could borrow the money. My dependence was solely on the Lord of glory.

Soon, my faith actions and words were interrupted by a knock on the door.

I opened the door to find a friendly-looking man on my doorstep. He identified himself as someone who had been sent to my house by the telegraph office. He said, "They would have called you, but you have no phone. I'm here to inform you that money has been wired to you at the telegraph office, but you must come down to sign for it."

My pulse quickened. I could hardly keep the excitement out of my voice. "How much money?" I asked.

The man replied, "I have no idea. I'm just here to deliver the message. I suggest you come down to the office as soon as you can."

I thanked him and turned my expressions to thanksgiving to the Lord for acting to meet my need for a car payment.

In less than half an hour, two men from the finance company were at my door. Before they could open their mouths to speak even one negative word, I exultantly announced, "Hey, guys, I've got your money."

They looked surprised. "You do?"

"Well," I clarified, "I don't have the money right at hand, but it has been wired to me at the telegraph office. I must go down and sign for it. I have only one problem. My wife is away for the afternoon, and I'm caring for my small children. If you would stay here with my four kids, I'll go get the money."

They looked a little shell-shocked.

"Okay. If you go get the money, we'll stay here with your children. It's a little unusual that we should have to babysit to make our collection. But, if you can get the money, we'll do the babysitting."

I went to the telegraph office to sign for the mysterious money sent from someone, somewhere. I didn't have the slightest clue who had sent it or how much it was. I just knew it was the Lord's provision, and it would be sufficient to make my car payment that day.

I needed seventy-five dollars for the payment. I received one hundred fifty dollars.

Sometime later, I learned how it all had come to pass. A man more than six hundred miles away had heard the voice of the Lord saying, *Send Don Gossett one hundred fifty dollars.* So, he sat down to write out a check to mail to me, but the Lord spoke again, saying, *Don't mail it to him. He needs it right now. Wire the money to him.*

I thank God for people who can hear the voice of the Lord and obey it. That man did so.

By speaking Philippians 4:19 with conviction and faith, I spoke into existence an awesome miracle that day. But nothing happened until I spoke His Word.

As I relive that day in my memory, I remember the words of the Lord Jesus:

> But I say unto you, that every idle word that men shall speak, they shall give account thereof in the day of judgment. For by thy words thou shalt be justified, and by thy words thou shalt be condemned. (Matthew 12:36–37)

43

THE CHILDREN'S BREAD

E. W. Kenyon

In the gospel of Mark, we find the beautiful story of Jesus dealing with the Syro-Phoenician woman. It includes one of the most striking expressions that ever fell from the Master's lips.

Jesus was on a sort of vacation, trying to get away from the crowds to spend time with His disciples.

> And from thence he arose, and went into the borders of Tyre and Sidon, and entered into an house, and would have no man know it: but he could not be hid. For a certain woman, whose young daughter had an unclean spirit, heard of him, and came and fell at his feet: the woman was a Greek, a Syrophenician by nation; and she besought him that he would cast forth the devil out of her daughter. (Mark 7:24–26)

Jesus answered, saying, "Let the children first be filled: for it is not meet to take the children's bread, and to cast it unto the dogs" (verse 27).

Not to be put off, the woman replied, *"Yes, Lord: yet the dogs under the table eat of the children's crumbs"* (verse 28).

This touched Jesus's heart. He simply said, *"Go thy way; the devil is gone out of thy daughter"* (verse 29).

The woman was a Gentile. She knew she had no right to seek help from this prophet, a rabbi who was ministering to the lost sheep of the house of Israel.

But Jesus said something of great importance. He said, *"It is not meet to take the children's bread."*

Have you even thought of healing in such terms? *"The children's bread."*

Every child has the right to bread—the right to eat. In the same way, every child of God who is sick has a right to his or her own *"children's bread."*

This puts healing on a new and intensely practical plane.

44

AFTER HANDS HAVE BEEN LAID UPON YOU

Don Gossett

You've acted on Jesus's words:

> *And these signs shall follow them that believe; In my name shall they cast out devils; they shall speak with new tongues; they shall take up serpents; and if they drink any deadly thing, it shall not hurt them; they shall lay hands on the sick, and they shall recover.* (Mark 16:17–18)

You can have great assurance that there will be a performance of what Jesus has promised, for He watches over His Word to perform it. (See Jeremiah 1:12 ASV.) This is a very positive promise. Jesus did not say, "You might recover," or "I hope that you will recover," or "Some might possibly recover." No! Without reservation, Jesus declared, *"They shall recover."*

As a believer, you can lay your own hands upon yourself for healing, or you can utilize the hands of other believers. If you do not receive an instantaneous miracle, do not cast away confidence.

When Jesus walked this earth, He healed people in various ways. Many were healed instantly, and yet, other people were healed gradually. Whether you are healed in the moment or a gradual mending process has begun, you can go your way, praising Him with confidence that He is keeping His Word with you.

Begin to confess it: "I am recovering. Jesus said so, and I believe His Word. I am not relying on how I look, how I feel, or how others think I look. I have accepted Jesus's Word at face value. I am recovering!"

James 1 declares that when you ask God for anything, you must ask in faith, without wavering.

> *For he that wavereth is like a wave of the sea driven with the wind and tossed. For let not that man think that he shall receive any thing of the Lord.* (James 1:6–7)

"Any thing" includes healing. Your role in this drama of faith is to possess unwavering confidence that the Lord will keep His Word. If you waver in your faith, then you deny yourself the Lord's healing. Do not waver in your confession of faith: "By His stripes, I am healed." (See Isaiah 53:5 NKJV.)

Until your healing is fully manifested, you are engaged in a fight of faith. It is not a fight against God or His Word but a fight against the thief, who comes *"to steal, and to kill, and to destroy"* (John 10:10). In this conflict, use the weapons of your warfare, which are mighty through God for the pulling down of satanic strongholds. (See 2 Corinthians 10:4.)

You may wonder, *Should I continue to have hands laid upon me until my healing is fully manifested?* That is not necessary. It would likely be prompted by unbelief, which would totally defeat your purpose. Healing comes through acting on the Word of Jesus. Once is quite enough.

Act like you are recovering. Begin to do things you could not do before. Praise the Lord that you are recovering. When others inquire about your condition, simply tell them that you are recovering, thanks be to God.

Make no mistake, the devil doesn't want you to recover. Here's how to deal with him. Declare, "Satan, I resist you in the name of Jesus. For it is written, *They shall lay hands on the sick, and they shall recover.* In Jesus's mighty name, I am recovering!"

Thousands of people have been healed through the ministry of the laying on of hands. What God has done for others, He is doing for you. Praise Him now for your recovery!

45

TAKE UP THY BED AND WALK

E. W. Kenyon

Now there is at Jerusalem by the sheep market a pool, which is called in the Hebrew tongue Bethesda, having five porches. In these lay a great multitude of impotent folk, of blind, halt, withered, waiting for the moving of the water....And a certain man was there, which had an infirmity thirty and eight years. When Jesus saw him lie, and knew that he had been now a long time in that case, he saith unto him, Wilt thou be made whole? The impotent man answered him, Sir, I have no man, when the water is troubled, to put me into the pool: but while I am coming, another steppeth down before me. Jesus saith unto him, Rise, take up thy bed, and walk. And immediately the man was made whole, and took up his bed, and walked.
(John 5:2–3, 5–9)

And, behold, a woman, which was diseased with an issue of blood twelve years, came behind him, and touched the hem of his garment: for she said within herself, If I may but touch his

> garment, I shall be whole. But Jesus turned him about, and when he saw her, he said, Daughter, be of good comfort; thy faith hath made thee whole. And the woman was made whole from that hour. (Matthew 9:20–22)

Some are always waiting for the waters to be stirred, waiting for someone else to come with the prayer of faith, waiting for someone else to take on the burden, waiting for someone else to believe for them, and waiting for someone else to study the Bible and get to know the Father for them.

Believing is simply acting on the Word. Jesus said, in effect, "Get up. Take your bed. Go home. Go to work."

To the woman, Jesus said, "*Thy faith hath made thee whole.*" That statement proves that we imprison ourselves in poverty, in want, in physical limitations, and in weakness by our own unbelief, our unwillingness to act on the Word of God.

In Jesus's name, we are healed. Our faith has done it—not the faith of Jesus, not the faith of somebody else. Our faith has made us whole, or else our unbelief has made us sick. We keep ourselves in poverty and want. We are living a life of weakness and want by our own volition.

No one can rob us of faith. No one can rob us of health. I can "believe myself" out of any prison in which circumstances may incarcerate me. I am linked with deity. So are you. We are children of God. His life is imparted to us. We are members of the body of Christ.

You haven't any right to be sick or held in bondage, because Jesus has purchased complete redemption for you. You have yielded to sin and disease and circumstances. You have been neutral. You have become a floating atom on the sea of pain and misery. Rebel against it. Take up arms against it. Join the ranks of Jesus. Say, "From this hour, Satan, your dominion over me is ended." Rebel against Satan's dominion.

Your bondage is not the will of love.

Your disease is not God's policeman to correct your behavior.

Disease is of the devil.

Poverty is of the devil.

That broken heart, that wrecked life, is not of God.

Rebel against it. Take your deliverance.

In [Christ Jesus] *we have redemption through his blood, the forgiveness of sins, according to the riches of his grace.*
(Ephesians 1:7)

This covers your case absolutely. Take up your bed and walk. Pick up your circumstances and walk off without them. Declare to them, "I am your master. I have conquered you. I am an overcomer."

Believing the Word means acting upon it. Passivity is the soil where sickness grows. Nonaction is unbelief. When you do not act, you consent to the action of disease, the action of Satan. Refuse to be in bondage any longer. No matter how long your bondage has lasted, it cannot kill the ability to act.

Jesus said to that man, *"Rise, take up thy bed, and walk."*

This man had to form a new type of thinking. He had to awaken. He had to develop new habits of thinking.

Make yourself act on the Word. Take up your pain, no matter what it is, and walk. In Jesus's name, take your place among the victors. You are a partaker of God's nature and of His life. The same mighty Spirit dwells in you that dwelled in the apostles Paul and John. The same Spirit that raised Jesus from the dead is yours. Take your place.

46

WHEN JESUS RAISED A BOY FROM THE DEAD

Don Gossett

Jesus answered and said unto them, Go and show John again those things which ye do hear and see: the blind receive their sight, and the lame walk, the lepers are cleansed, and the deaf hear, the dead are raised up, and the poor have the gospel preached to them. (Matthew 11:4–5)

There are three specific references to Jesus raising a person from the dead:

1. When raising Lazarus in John 11, Jesus said, *"Lazarus, come forth"* (verse 43).

2. When raising the widow's son in Luke 7, Jesus said, *"Young man, I say unto thee, Arise"* (verse 14).

3. When raising Jairus' daughter in Luke 8, Jesus said, *"Maid, arise"* (verse 54).

Often, I hear reports of, or witness myself, the miracles of God's healing power: the blind see, the deaf hear, cancers are destroyed, and more. It's a rare occurrence, however, to hear of the dead being raised, even though it has been documented many times in the twentieth century and continues to happen in the twenty-first century.

Throughout our years in ministry, the Lord of the harvest has sent my wife, Debra, and me to many of the cities and villages of India to minister the gospel. When we arrived for our crusade in Jabalpur, Madya Pradesh, in northern India, we were informed by the organizers that we shouldn't expect large crowds. They explained, "Unlike your ministry in southern India, where you preach to tens of thousands, it is very difficult here in the north. We have never had more than five hundred people at any event."

The first night of the crusade, there were about a thousand people present, which caused a sense of excitement among the pastors and leaders. As I was preaching, and as my message was being translated by my interpreter, there came a disturbance in the crowd. Most of the people were seated on the ground. A man and a woman stood up, and the man held a small child, lying limply. The couple had a look of deep anxiety on their faces. They began to shake the child vigorously, while another woman poured water on him. Suddenly, the parents rushed toward the platform. The father dropped to his knees with his son in his arms, wailing in Hindi. My interpreter translated what he was saying: "My child is dead! My child is dead!"

Crusade workers gathered around the family, including one from our crusade team, Dr. Daniels, who assessed that the child had stopped breathing and had no pulse. He was not responding to any kind of stimulus. Medically speaking, he was dead. The crusade chairman, David Lai, came to the platform to inform our coworker, Brother Manohar, "The child is dead. Should we quietly take the parents and child away to the hospital?"

Instead, Brother Manohar responded, "We will have prayer." He asked me to agree with him in prayer. I asked the audience to stand and stretch forth their hands toward the little boy as the Lord anointed me to pray a strong prayer of faith. Thirty seconds later, there was a shout of praise from the workers surrounding the boy. A great buzz of excitement swept through the crowd. Brother Manohar was absolutely beaming when he returned to the platform and gave me this report: "This little boy was dead for several minutes. Dr. Daniels confirmed he was dead. Jesus Christ touched him, and now, he's alive!"

The next morning, the boy's mother brought him to meet Debra and me. He who had been pronounced dead was indeed very much alive! His mother was smiling sweetly when we met her.

Word spread like wildfire throughout that Hindu community: "A boy has been raised from the dead by the power of Jesus Christ!"

On the second night in Jabalpur, more than ten thousand people were present. I explained to the audience, "I know you are here because a little boy was raised from the dead last night. It's not the raising of that boy from the dead, however, that will bring you salvation through Christ. You must believe that Jesus was crucified, buried, and raised from the grave on the third day and confess Him as your only Lord and Savior."

As I always did throughout my twenty years of ministry in India, I led the people in this prayer: "I renounce all other gods and goddesses. I will forsake all my idols. I receive Jesus Christ as my personal Savior—the Lord of my life."

After that prayer, I asked those present, "If you have received Jesus Christ as your Lord, please raise both hands in surrender to Him." Most of those thousands of people raised their hands!

Praise the Lord, the miracle had attracted the people to attend the service, but it was the message of the gospel that brought them salvation.

I am not ashamed of the gospel of Christ: for it is the power of God unto salvation to every one that believeth.
(Romans 1:16)

47

STRETCHING FORTH A WITHERED HAND

Don Gossett

And, behold, there was a man which had his hand withered.... Then saith [Jesus] to the man, Stretch forth thine hand. And he stretched it forth; and it was restored whole, like as the other. (Matthew 12:10, 13)

Does Jesus still heal withered hands? Yes, for He is *"Jesus Christ the same yesterday, and to day, and for ever"* (Hebrews 13:8).

I was ministering at an open-air crusade in the heart of Montreal, Quebec. People walking by would stop and listen to the singing and the preaching. One particular man sat there, chain-smoking all the time. He was not disrespectful but was simply unaware of the sanctity of a gospel service. Watching and listening to the testimonies of people who were healed seemed to interest him keenly. He came forward to ask me to pray for him. I asked, "What is your need for healing?" He said, "My left hand is withered I ask your prayers for healing this hand."

I shared with him about the man in Jesus's day who had a withered hand, and about the fact that Jesus healed the man by simply saying, *"Stretch forth thine hand."* In doing so, Jesus spoke into existence an awesome miracle. But nothing happened until Jesus spoke those words.

I touched the man's hand; it was like stone. He had no ability to use it. In the name of Jesus, I spoke for healing of that man's withered hand and the Lord restored it! I handed him my large Bible to hold in his left hand. Enthusiastically he grasped the Bible, lifted it up, and began waving it with the once deformed hand, a demonstration of the miracle he had received. That man returned to our crusade the next several nights. When I would invite him to come forward and demonstrate what the Lord had done, he was eager to do so!

There was another man in one of those next services who was particularly interested in the Lord's healing power. He explained to me, "I have a son at home who is deaf in both ears. I will bring him to the next service for prayers that his deaf ears would be opened."

The following night, the man brought his son. What a delight it was to speak in the name of Jesus and command his deafness to depart. Afterward, when I tested his hearing, he was overwhelmed with the joy that he could finally hear! His father also returned to our crusade during the evenings that followed. I would stand behind the boy and softly whisper, and he would repeat my words with accuracy. I would hold a small wristwatch to his ears to demonstrate that he could now hear the ticking. Both miracles—healing of the withered hand and opening dear ears—were evidences of the authority of the name of Jesus! But nothing happened until the name of Jesus was spoken.

48

A THORN DISLODGED FROM A THROAT

Don Gossett

There came a leper to him, beseeching him, and kneeling down to him, and saying unto him, If thou wilt, thou canst make me clean. And Jesus, moved with compassion, put forth his hand, and touched him, and saith unto him, I will; be thou clean. And as soon as he had spoken, immediately the leprosy departed from him, and he was cleansed. And he straitly charged him, and forthwith sent him away; and saith unto him, See thou say nothing to any man: but go thy way, show thyself to the priest, and offer for thy cleansing those things which Moses commanded, for a testimony unto them. But he went out, and began to publish it much, and to blaze abroad the matter, insomuch that Jesus could no more openly enter into the city, but was without in desert places: and they came to him from every quarter. (Mark 1:40–45)

In many cases of miracles, the combination of touching and speaking is found. Jesus both touched the leper and spoke a healing word to him. Perhaps more significant was the spoken word: *"As soon as he had spoken, immediately the leprosy departed from him, and he was cleansed."*

The morning after the close of a Miracle Life Crusade in Trivandrum, India, we met with the other pastors at a breakfast given by a local government official, who rose to speak, saying, "I went over the entire stadium and grounds last night. With my associates, we estimate that there was a crowd of no less than one hundred fifty thousand people."

Many miraculous stories were shared about the crusade. One unusual testimony concerned a woman who had accidentally swallowed a thorn that had lodged in her throat, causing bleeding and much pain. She had seen a doctor, who had taken X-rays and offered to perform a medical procedure in which he would slit open her throat to remove the thorn. This woman was poor, however, and the procedure was to cost the equivalent of around thirty-five dollars, a sum she could never pay. Her only option was to continue suffering.

During one evening of the crusade, the Holy Spirit gave me a word of knowledge. Obeying what I had heard, I stood up and said, "There is a lady here with a critical throat problem. Please stand up, place your hand on your throat, and receive your miracle in Jesus's name."

Seeing the woman standing with a hand on her throat, I asked her to speak. She said, "My throat is healed in Jesus's name."

Then, I commanded her to repeat three times the word *swallow*. In that moment, she swallowed, dislodging the thorn from her throat. She said, "Swallow, swallow, swallow!" A poor woman had received a miracle. Perhaps it was not as spectacular as a blind person receiving his sight or a crippled limb being healed, but, for that desperate woman, it was a wonder of God that brought immense delight into her life!

49

HEALING A RAGING FEVER

Don Gossett

He arose out of the synagogue, and entered into Simon's house. And Simon's wife's mother was taken with a great fever; and they besought him for her. And he stood over her, and rebuked the fever; and it left her: and immediately she arose and ministered unto them. (Luke 4:38–39)

A raging fever is evidence of infection. By speaking words of rebuke, Jesus spoke into existence a body free from fever. But, once again, nothing happened until Jesus spoke the words of rebuke.

Some years ago, my wife was stricken with rheumatic fever. Her skin was discolored, and her body had swollen to an abnormal size. The intensity of the pain of this fever was so severe that even the touch of a sheet to her body was more than she could bear. Her condition reached a climax one afternoon when she attempted to go to the bathroom unaided. It was something she hadn't done for many days. I was away from her for a short time, caring for one of our children. When I returned to her room, her bed was empty. I called out, but there was no reply. As anxiety gripped my heart, I quickly made my way through the house to the bathroom, where I found her unconscious. I knelt beside her still form, not certain whether she was dead or alive. The inspired words of Luke 4 raced through my mind—words describing how Jesus *"rebuked the fever"* of Simon's mother-in-law.

Likewise, in Jesus's name, I boldly rebuked the fever that seemed bent on taking my wife from me. I spoke into existence the release of the fever's death hold on her body. As it was with Jesus at Simon's house, nothing happened until I spoke the word of authority.

She opened her eyes and began to speak, saying, "Don, while you were speaking, the Lord gave me a vision. He showed me that healing streams will flow from your hands whenever you lay your hands on sick people."

I carried her back to her bed. Within two days, she was miraculously raised up and made completely whole. Her healing of rheumatic fever was complete.

I challenge you: confess the Word concerning your healing. As you do, believe and proclaim that God's Word will not return void but will accomplish what it says it will. (See Isaiah 55:10–11.) Believe in the name of Jesus, and you will be healed, according to 1 Peter 2:24: *"By* [His] *stripes ye were healed."* This is affirmed by Matthew 8:17: "[Jesus] *Himself took our infirmities, and bare our sicknesses."*

Refuse to tolerate any symptoms. The Word you speak is alive and full of power. As you speak the healing Scriptures, walk out of the realm of sickness and into the arena of health and wholeness. It happened for Simon's mother-in-law, and it happened for my wife, enabling her to walk in divine health for the next thirty years of her life.

You, too, can boldly exercise the "believer's rebuke." Declare it boldly: "I rebuke you, Satan, in the name of Jesus!" Be bold, and great forces will come to your aid. Your problem may not be fever; it may be cancer, heart trouble, diabetes, high blood pressure, or something else. Whatever the issue, refuse to be Satan's dumping ground. Be fearless as you rebuke the devil's oppressions.

50

HEALED OF CANCER

Don Gossett

During a service in which I was ministering, ten people were present who had once been stricken with cancer but were miraculously healed by God's power. What God has done for those ten, He can do for those of you who suffer from the same affliction. And if God can heal ten, then He can heal one hundred more—and even more. More important, God can heal you!

First, realize that God is not the author of cancer.

Every good gift and every perfect gift is from above, and cometh down from the Father of lights, with whom is no variableness, neither shadow of turning. (James 1:17)

Anyone who has ever been stricken with cancer knows that it could never be regarded as a *"good…and perfect gift."* Often, cancer is associated with a foul stench, and it generally produces excruciating pain to the victim. Malignant cancers result in eventual death. Indeed, cancer remains one of the most terrifying threats to human health and welfare.

First Timothy 6:17 says, *"Trust...in the living God, who giveth us richly all things to enjoy."* The devil, not God, is the one who wants you to suffer and experience oppression. God is the Giver of all good things for us to enjoy. No cancer victim can rightfully say that he or she enjoys suffering. Let's be sure of this one fact: God is *not* the author of cancer.

It is important for you to realize that cancer is an oppression of the devil. Sickness, disease, and infirmities are in this world because of the devil's power, but Jesus came for this very purpose: to destroy the works of the devil.

> *For this purpose the Son of God was manifested, that he might destroy the works of the devil.* (1 John 3:8)

Cancer is one of the works of the devil that Jesus came to destroy with His life-giving power. Contrast the work of Satan, the destroyer, to Jesus Christ, the Giver of life.

> *The thief cometh not, but for to steal, and to kill, and to destroy: I am come that they might have life, and that they might have it more abundantly.* (John 10:10)

In this passage of Scripture, Jesus clearly unmasked the devil for the thief, killer, and destroyer that he is. Satan is the one who causes that diabolical oppression of cancer. But Jesus is the Giver of abundant life.

> *God anointed Jesus of Nazareth with the Holy Ghost and with power: who went about doing good, and healing all that were oppressed of the devil; for God was with him.* (Acts 10:38)

This Scripture clearly reveals that any sickness Jesus encountered when He walked the earth was the work of the devil. Jesus came to minister to all who were oppressed by the devil's schemes, and He does so today, because *"Jesus Christ [is] the same yesterday, and today, and forever"* (Hebrews 13:8 NKJV).

THE NAME THAT DISPELS CANCER

The power over the devil's oppression of cancer is found in the mighty name of Jesus. In Acts 3, the apostle Peter explained to an astonished crowd how a lame man had received a miraculous healing.

> *And [Jesus's] name through faith in [his] name hath made this man strong, whom ye see and know: yea, the faith which is by him hath given him this perfect soundness in the presence of you all.* (Acts 3:16)

It was by the power of the name of Jesus that the lame man was healed. So it is today that we take authority and dominion over the devil's oppression in the name of Jesus.

I often wonder how people react as they listen to my radio broadcasts and hear the testimonies of miraculous healings. I suppose some may think that those testimonies are examples of fanaticism or that we are living under some mystical cloud. No, my friend, this is blessed reality. Never will I forget the first time I began to exercise the dominion of Jesus's name against cancer. A great anointing and holy thrill swept through my being as I approached the cancer cases and spoke in the name of Jesus. Remember, Jesus said, *"Whatsoever ye shall ask in my name, that will I do, that the Father may be glorified in the Son"* (John 14:13).

THE YOKE BREAKER

Know that the anointing of the Holy Spirit is given to us to loosen every yoke of bondage. The Bible says that *"the yoke shall be destroyed because of the anointing"* (Isaiah 10:27). At the beginning of His ministry, Jesus pronounced,

> *The Spirit of the Lord is upon me, because he hath anointed me to preach the gospel to the poor; he hath sent me to heal the brokenhearted, to preach deliverance to the captives, and recovering of sight to the blind, to set at liberty them that are bruised, to preach the acceptable year of the Lord.*
>
> (Luke 4:18–19)

My friend, it was the anointing of the Holy Spirit in Jesus's life that enabled Him to be the Liberator of the devil's captives. And it is this same anointing that has been given to us so that we might minister deliverance to every captive of cancer.

Remember, "*God is no respecter of persons*" (Acts 10:34). In other words, God does not play favorites. As He has healed so many other people of cancer by His unlimited power, He can also heal you!

RIGHT AND WRONG ATTITUDES

I have discovered three attitudes that people have regarding God's healing of cancer.

1. God can heal cancer, but He won't heal me.
2. God can heal cancer, and He might heal me.
3. God can heal cancer, and He will heal *my* cancer!

God is not only able but also willing to heal you. In fact, it is His will to heal you!

WHAT TO DO TO BE HEALED OF CANCER

Prepare your heart by searching it to see if there is any unconfessed sin. Put away the practice of any sinful living, for sin in your heart will bind the arm of God on your behalf. Also examine your heart to see if there is any attitude of unforgiveness, for a spirit of unforgiveness is also a blockade to God's power.

Follow the prescription found in James 4:6–8:

God resisteth the proud, but giveth grace unto the humble. Submit yourselves therefore to God. Resist the devil, and he will flee from you. Draw nigh to God, and he will draw nigh to you.

After you have prepared your heart by removing all hindrances to receiving healing from the Lord, begin to meditate on what Jesus Christ died to provide for you. Consider His bleeding stripes. Praise God for offering His Son for your deliverance.

Think on Matthew 8:17: "[Jesus] *Himself took our infirmities, and bare our sicknesses."* Realize what that means for your life. Jesus Himself took your infirmities and bore your sicknesses so that you could be free.

Ponder Isaiah 53:5: *"With his stripes we are healed."* Consider the virtue of those bleeding stripes and how your healing has already been purchased through the provision of Jesus Christ.

Praise God for 1 Peter 2:24: *"By* [Jesus's] *stripes ye were healed."* Give praise to God that your healing is already an accomplished fact.

Meditate once again on Hebrews 13:8: *"Jesus Christ* [is] *the same yesterday, and to day, and for ever."* The same Christ who healed when He walked on this earth still heals today—right now! Believe it and receive His deliverance.

Pray as you are instructed in James 5:15: *"The prayer of faith shall save the sick, and the Lord shall raise him up."*

Praise God for these scriptural truths that can set you free and heal you of any diabolical cancer Satan has sent against you. Resist it in the name of Jesus. Praise the Lord Jesus for His bleeding stripes. Be made whole in His power!

PART IV
KEYS TO OVERCOMING

51

A VICTORIOUS CONFESSION

Don Gossett

In the school of Christ, you learn to say, "*Thanks be unto God, which always causeth us to triumph…*" (2 Corinthians 2:14). In the school of Satan, you learned a neutral, or negative, confession. And that neutral confession will bring you down to Satan's dominion and keep you there. Your life will be a constant struggle. You will become a preacher of unbelief, doubt, and fear.

Learn to say, with fearlessness, "*God is our refuge and strength, a very present help in trouble*" (Psalm 46:1).

> *Fear thou not; for I am with thee: be not dismayed; for I am thy God: I will strengthen thee; yea, I will help thee; yea, I will uphold thee with the right hand of my righteousness.*
> (Isaiah 41:10)

That is victory. That is the declaration of the Conqueror. That is a positive testimony that will shake the foundation of hell. That truth brings glory to the Father, joy to the Son, and victory to our own spirits.

As you maintain your solid stance, your testimony becomes richer and more helpful. The living Word becomes a part of your very being. Now, you are acting on and speaking the Word that lives in you, that is becoming a part of you. You are now bearing the fruits of righteousness.

Now he that ministereth seed to the sower both minister bread for your food, and multiply your seed sown, and increase the fruits of your righteousness. (2 Corinthians 9:10)

52

BEING INDEPENDENT OF CIRCUMSTANCES

E. W. Kenyon

The Father never intended for any of His children to be in bondage to circumstances or to other people. Not only has He redeemed them out of the hand of Satan, but He also has given them His own nature, His own ability, so that they become masters instead of slaves. They were destined to be the controlling element of every force in the world.

> *I have learned, in whatsoever state I am, therewith to be content. I know both how to be abased, and I know how to abound: every where and in all things I am instructed both to be full and to be hungry, both to abound and to suffer need.*
> (Philippians 4:11–12)

We dare to face life's problems with a fearless spirit.

> *Now thanks be unto God, which always causeth us to triumph in Christ.* (2 Corinthians 2:14)

This was Paul's experience. Whether he was in jail or on a ship in the midst of a storm that threatened ultimate destruction, he was fearless because he was linked up with omnipotence.

We ought to remember Proverbs 3:5–6: *"Trust in the Lord with all thine heart; and lean not unto thine own understanding. In all thy ways acknowledge him, and he shall direct thy paths."*

How many times men are driven to extremities where their own wisdom and ability are of no avail! Then, they cast all their anxiety and care upon Him, for He cares for them. (See 1 Peter 5:7.) We come to our wits' end, and we know not what step to take. Then, He becomes our light and our deliverance.

Jesus said, *"I am the light of the world: he that followeth me shall not walk in darkness, but shall have the light of life"* (John 8:12). This is a new kind of light. It is wisdom. It is ability. It is the thing that Jesus had in His earth walk that made Him the most outstanding Man who ever lived.

There has never been a time when the heart of man has needed inward light as it needs it now. Our reasoning faculties, which find all their resources in the five senses, have limitations that give us a sense of failure, an inferiority complex. It is then that this inward light of the Spirit becomes our only guide. Now, we should cultivate that inward light! We should learn to depend on it because it is so much safer than our reasoning faculties.

"The Lord is my shepherd; I shall not want" (Psalm 23:1). I like to put that verse in the present tense: "The Lord is my shepherd; I do not want." He is my Shepherd. He is the One who has guaranteed my protection and care, so that, in the presence of my enemies, I may feast in perfect security.

Our God is bigger, greater, and wiser than any of our enemies. We can fearlessly trust in Him.

> *The LORD is my light and my salvation; whom shall I fear? The LORD is the strength of my life; of whom shall I be afraid?*
> (Psalm 27:1)

You and God are linked together. Remember that, in every danger, He is the strength of your life; He is your ability. My heart comes back to 2 Corinthians 3:5: "*Our sufficiency is of God.*" That means your ability, your wisdom, is from Him. That makes you superior to your circumstances. It makes you superior to physical weakness. You are in touch with God. You and God are bound to each other.

> *Fear thou not; for I am with thee: be not dismayed; for I am thy God: I will strengthen thee; yea, I will help thee; yea, I will uphold thee with the right hand of my righteousness.*
> (Isaiah 41:10)

God wants you to know that He is your God, no matter the opposition. No matter what the danger may be, He is yours, and you are His. He will guide you and keep His eye upon you. He will shield you from every danger.

Those who would harm you can't touch you. "*A thousand shall fall at thy side, and ten thousand at thy right hand; but it shall not come nigh thee*" (Psalm 91:7). You are under the Lord's protection. Rest in Him with utter abandonment; trust Him with joyful confidence. He will never fail you.

53

HALLELUJAH LIVING

Don Gossett

Are you troubled? Are you disheartened? Are you worried about the future? These days, the worldwide economic downturn seems to be in the headline of every newscast and newspaper article.

Well, hallelujah! We don't have to live that way. The discouraging, depressing perspective of the secular world we live in does not apply to the people of God. God's Word is always true, powerful, and effective, regardless of the circumstances of our daily lives.

> *Man shall not live by bread alone, but by every word that proceeds from the mouth of God.* (Matthew 4:4)

Let me relate the true story of a victorious woman I know.

Pauline Kasara faced the bleakest of futures. Her husband had killed himself in their home in Uganda. According to tribal law, everything she had—her children, her estate, and her savings—was to go to her late husband's family. Pauline would be left destitute and alone.

Even though she was devastated by the discovery of her husband's body, Pauline knew that she had to act swiftly and prayerfully if she wanted to be the one to raise her children. To avoid the plight of other Ugandan widows, she hurried to the local bank and withdrew all available funds before the authorities discovered her husband's death. When she returned home, she quickly gathered every valuable that she could pack into her car and drove to her children's school to discreetly collect them from their classrooms. Pauline and her children fled over the border to Kenya, where the unjust laws of Uganda could not reach them. They became refugees.

With the moderate amount of money she had brought with her, hardworking and resourceful Pauline set up a small business in the heart of Nairobi. She designed and created African garments to sell to the thousands of tourists who flocked to Kenya each year to go on safari.

Filled with deep gratitude and humility that she had managed to escape Uganda with her children, Pauline made a heartfelt promise to the Lord. She said, "God, I will tithe on every dollar of sales that comes into my business. I will bring it to the storehouse at the end of each workday because I know that You will bless me." Pauline called it "going into partnership with God."

At the end of each business day, Pauline counted her daily receipts and made a trip to her church. She didn't bring 10 percent of her *net* profits but 10 percent of her entire *gross* sales. Soon, God began to bless and prosper Pauline in an extraordinary way.

Two years after Pauline's dramatic exodus from Uganda, I came to Kenya for meetings at her church, where Pastor Dennis White, a longtime friend and associate, told me of this most remarkable woman and the tremendous blessing she had been to their church. He invited me to his home to meet this radiant woman. Sitting on the patio of his home, Pauline related her wonderful testimony in her own words. What a blessing and encouragement to hear her story!

When we travel overseas to minister in other nations, we go knowing that we will cover our expenses with the financial help of our generous friends and partners in North America. We do not expect any monetary compensation. Rather, we are thrilled for the opportunity to sow spiritual seeds into their community and nation. So, imagine my surprise when, at the end of our conversation, Pauline offered to give a gift to our ministry! "Oh, Pauline," I said, "I can't accept that. We come to Africa to give, not to receive!"

"But Pastor Gossett," Pauline replied, "would you limit my blessing from the Lord by not taking my gift?"

What else could I do but gratefully receive the small brown envelope that she placed in my hands? Later, in the privacy of my room, I opened the envelope and was amazed to discover twenty-five hundred U.S. dollars! By African standards, that was a fortune. Before the meetings came to an end, Pauline sowed another gift that paid to print 95,000 pieces of Christian literature for Kenya.

Pauline practiced what she called "Hallelujah Giving," which mirrored the principles of giving set out in Malachi 3:10:

> *Bring ye all the tithes into the storehouse, that there may be meat in mine house, and prove me now herewith, saith the LORD of hosts, if I will not open you the windows of heaven, and pour you out a blessing, that there shall not be room enough to receive it.*

I call it "Hallelujah Living."

Recently, one of our ministry partners, a saleswoman working on commission, began saying a quiet "Hallelujah" for increased sales at work each time she passed the cash register. Her sales have taken off, and she thanks God, as well as continues to say "Hallelujah" each time she goes past the cash register.

An unemployed carpenter in Regina, Saskatchewan, related to me that he immediately found a job when he began to practice "Hallelujah Living." Another man, in Tulsa, Oklahoma, had been laid off from a large plant but took the faith position of "Hallelujah Living." Soon, by a miracle, a job was opened to him.

You can break the curse over your finances by agreeing with what God says in His Word, which tells us that He is our Provider. However, if you have become accustomed to speaking doubtful words about the Lord's provision, you will be defeated in the financial arenas of your life. Instead, declare, "Hallelujah, my God supplies all my need!"

God created His world with words, and He gives each of us the same privilege. Saying things like, "I can't pay my bills" or "I will never have enough money to meet my needs" will keep you in the bonds of poverty. On the other hand, faith-filled words and actions will move mountains of debt.

When our grandson, Brandon Gossett, was a little boy, if someone asked him his name, he would earnestly reply, "My name is Brandon Sockett."

I would then say, "Well, if your name is Brandon Sockett, then you can call me 'Grandpa Sockett.' We'll 'sock it' to the devil!"

That's an important aspect of our Christian life: commanding him who is called the thief (see John 10:10) to take his hands off of your soul, your body, and your money. Words that resist the devil are also words that move mountains. Do it now: sock it to the devil in the name of Jesus!

54

TITHING YOUR MIRACLE

Don Gossett

I want to share a principle that creates miracles for me and can do the same for you, too. The principle is tithing. Tithing is the best-kept secret to prosperity. It's a time-tested Bible truth that works today, yet it has been neglected by many believers.

To those who are in relationship with the Lord, tithing is an acknowledgment that He truly owns everything. He has commanded us to return tithes and offerings to Him. In response, He rebukes the devourer for our sakes, opens heaven's windows, and pours out overflowing blessings.

We don't think about money the same way God does. Tithing can be a sensitive subject. Sometimes, ministers are afraid to speak about tithing to their congregations because they neither believe God's Word on the subject nor practice the principle themselves. Therefore, they cannot speak about it with conviction or give testimony from their own experiences.

Miracles never cease to amaze me. I expect them, but their consistent arrival is always delightful to experience. God said that on earth, there will always be the seasons of *"seedtime and harvest"* (Genesis 8:22). *"Seedtime"* is tithing time. The apostle Paul taught us the law of sowing and reaping: *"Do not be deceived, God is not mocked; for whatever a man sows, that he will also reap"* (Galatians 6:7). If you give with the confidence that you will receive a blessing, as promised by the Bible—a multiplied return—then you will have it.

As a tither, you automatically become solution-oriented rather than one who is focused on only the problem at hand. As a tither, you fix your heart on the Lord and trust in Him alone.

A Christian brother named Chip was down to his last thirty-five cents. He had a wife and a baby to feed and no hope of earning any money. With tears in his eyes, he beat his fists against the steering wheel of his car, asking, "God, what should I do?" God's Word arose in his heart and reminded him to tithe. He figured thirty-five cents would not even buy milk for his baby, so, he immediately went to a church and prayerfully put all of it into the offering plate.

As he walked out of the church, the Holy Spirit told him to solicit a job at a nearby office. He did and was hired immediately. In fact, his new employer gave him an advance on his earnings in the amount of two hundred dollars, which put food on the family's table that night. Chip reestablished his self-esteem as a provider for his family. Since then, he has remained a disciplined and committed tither.

Your needs exist to be met, not to intimidate, embarrass, and harass you. The Bible gives us a guarantee that God is our Source: *"My God shall supply all your need according to his riches in glory by Christ Jesus"* (Philippians 4:19). Speaking this verse, coupled with tithing, has been one of the keys to financial provision for me and my house for many years.

> *Give, and it shall be given unto you; good measure, pressed down, and shaken together, and running over, shall men give into your bosom. For with the same measure that ye mete withal it shall be measured to you again.* (Luke 6:38)

Notice that, according to this passage, whatever you receive is multiplied by what you give.

55

THINKING YOURSELF INTO SUCCESS

E. W. Kenyon

Criminals are not criminals by accident. Frequently, they think themselves into wrongdoing. They think about crime for so long that they lose any sense of its being wrong. Every form of wrongdoing is the product of wrong thinking.

It may take years for a man to destroy his own life, but he can do it. It is dreaming of doing something that shocks and horrifies at first but eventually becomes a familiar companion. This is what makes a criminal.

The same principle holds true in every department of life. The great musician has to live in the mental realm of music in order to be able to produce it. The great artist must live in the realm of great paintings. He or she dreams the picture first and then paints it from the imagination. The great architect mentally builds a bridge years before he or she ever creates the blueprints. The great novelist is first a dreamer who then puts that dream on paper.

We become that which we most intently think we are. Love is largely the work of the spirit through the imagination. A man thinks of a woman and dreams of her until she becomes a part of his dream life. Then, he is in love, and it becomes hard to live without her.

You dream of wealth until, after a while, your surroundings become unpleasant to you. You vow to do almost anything if it will allow you to achieve the life of which you have been dreaming.

If you wish to climb to the realm called success, it is imperative that you remember to master your dream life. You must absolutely govern your dreams. You must put your dream machinery to work on the right kind of fabric. Become the master of your dream life. You can dream for yourself a masterful personality, or you can dream a weak one. Out of your dreams will come either the masterful personality or the weaker one. If you will yourself to become a man or woman of influence, it can happen. Your career will be molded out of the things you dream.

Someone is going to become the great musician, the great statesman, the great lawyer, the great physician, or the great architect of the future. Why shouldn't it be you? Almost all of the truly great men and women of the world first carved their futures out of their dream lives, some of them even while they were surrounded by poverty and hardship. You can do the same!

56

POWER TO OVERCOME FIVE TYPES OF PAIN

Don Gossett

I often meet people who have tears streaming down their faces, their hearts burdened with indescribable hurts. God's Word will help us to overcome any problem or affliction that threatens to cause us pain. God's Word helps us to overcome our hurts! Here are just five types of affliction that can be overcome *"by the blood of the Lamb, and by the word of* [our] *testimony"* (Revelation 12:11).

1. EXTREME POVERTY

"At twelve-fifteen, God walked in the door." This is the testimony of a businessman named Charles. He had been a retail clothier for many years when adversity laid its blighting hand upon him. Plunged into extreme poverty, he was facing bankruptcy and total financial disaster that threatened not only his business but also his entire family. When the sad day came, he signed a writ of voluntary bankruptcy. Standing in his store while the creditor was invoicing his stock, he thanked God for so many years of financial blessing and success. In the end, however, all he had were memories. He was losing his store.

Suddenly, a man entered the shop, although Charles remembers it differently: "And then, at twelve-fifteen, God walked in the door. I say this reverently because, to me, it could have been none other than God in the person of my keenest competitor. He rarely came into my store. We were casual friends. He quietly reached into his pocket and handed me a sizable check, saying, 'Would this change the picture?' Stunned, and with tears in my eyes, I said, 'Yes, I'm quite sure it would.' Of all the acquaintances I had in the city, this man was the last person I would have expected to do a thing like that. My other friends felt sorry for me, but this man said he was sorry with 'money that talked.'"

Charles continued, "Who put it into that man's heart in my crucial hour? Nobody but God! The years that followed were successful and prosperous. And, with God's further help, I was able to pay my competitor back in full!"

Your poverty is likely much different from Charles'. However, you serve the same God as he did. God is your Source, the Supplier of all of your needs. Turn your double pains of poverty into double praise to the One of whom it is written, *"The* LORD *is my shepherd; I shall not want"* (Psalm 23:1).

2. LONELINESS

Are you lonely?

A man that hath friends must show himself friendly: and there is a friend that sticketh closer than a brother.
(Proverbs 18:24)

To have friends is important. Remember, God *"inhabitest the praises of Israel"* (Psalm 22:3). God lives in the place of praise. If you desire to experience God's presence, go to His address: Psalm

22:3. A sure way to overcome loneliness is to be possessed by the spirit of praise. God is never too busy to fellowship with you.

3. OVERWHELMING FEAR

What do you fear? The loss of a job? Illness or disease? Your children's future? Lack of finances? The threat of war? Death? Hell? Or worse?

Fear produces negative emotions and conditions, including torment, misery, defeat, destruction, and bondage. But you can stop the spirit of fear and live in true peace and confidence. As you study the Bible, you learn where fear comes from, so that you may tear down your insecurities and obtain freedom from their paralyzing effects. Discover for yourself how to conquer fear by speaking aloud these biblically based proclamations:

"God has not given me the spirit of fear!" (See 2 Timothy 1:7.)

"I will not fear what man can do to me!" (See Hebrews 13:6.)

As you speak these truths, you stand against fear and deny it any place to dwell in your heart.

4. PHYSICAL OR MENTAL TORMENT

Learning to overcome physical or mental torment calls for discipline.

In March 2010, I suffered from constant, chronic pain for many weeks due to an accident. Because of this, I have a new sense of compassion and understanding for those who have suffered from pain for long periods of time. The mental torment is a battle in the spiritual world. But, it is a battle we can win!

Like many believers, I pray for the sick whenever the opportunity arises. I have no doubt that one of the purposes of healing in Jesus's day, as well as in ours, was to get the attention of those who were lost so that they would come to know Him.

That is precisely what happened in my own family. My mother's miraculous recovery from a critical affliction was the convincing factor that brought my entire family to hear the gospel for the first time. Mother's miracle was "heaven's advertisement," attesting to the fact that Jesus is real and alive today and that He is still the Great Physician.

> [Jesus said,] *The Spirit of the Lord is upon me, because he hath anointed me to preach the gospel to the poor; he hath sent me to heal the brokenhearted, to preach deliverance to the captives, and recovering of sight to the blind, to set at liberty them that are bruised.* (Luke 4:18)

> *And in that same hour* [Jesus] *cured many of their infirmities and plagues, and of evil spirits; and unto many that were blind he gave sight. Then Jesus answering said unto* [the disciples of John the Baptist], *Go your way, and tell John what things ye have seen and heard; how that the blind see, the lame walk, the lepers are cleansed, the deaf hear, the dead are raised, to the poor the gospel is preached.* (Luke 7:21–22)

Based on my injury in 2010, I can say that it's no fun to be hurting. There's no joy in pain and discomfort. When God relieves a cold, stops a throbbing earache, restores strength to an accident victim, or cures cancer, it's all part of demonstrating His love for us. Isaiah prophesied about this when he foretold,

> [Jesus] *was wounded for our transgressions, he was bruised for our iniquities: the chastisement of our peace was upon him; and with his stripes we are healed.* (Isaiah 53:5)

Maybe you are battling an illness. Or, perhaps you are struggling as you watch a close friend or family member suffer. Questions and doubts may plague your mind. But the apostle James told us that *"the prayer of faith shall save the sick"* (James 5:15). I have personally experienced healing, and I have prayed for thousands to be healed. Some were healed; others were not. Nevertheless, Scripture is clear: I must trust the Word, pray for the sick, and expect God to perform the outcome. You'll be amazed at what God does when you give Him the opportunity. *"Lay hands on the sick, and they shall recover"* (Mark 16:18).

You can do that, in Jesus's name!

5. SORROW AND HEARTACHE

Based on my study of the Bible, I am convinced that if you are a believer, the happiest day of your life will be the day of your death.

> *We are confident, I say, and willing rather to be absent from the body, and to be present with the Lord.*
>
> (2 Corinthians 5:8)

> *For to me to live is Christ, and to die is gain.*
>
> (Philippians 1:21)

Someday, we all will die and depart to be with Jesus. It is our *"blessed hope"* (Titus 2:13) to be caught up in the rapture to be with the Lord Jesus forever. Are you living with the daily expectation that today could be the day?

The Holy Spirit put it into the heart of the apostle Paul:

> *Behold, I show you a mystery; we shall not all sleep, but we shall all be changed, in a moment, in the twinkling of an eye, at the last trump: for the trumpet shall sound, and the dead shall be raised incorruptible, and we shall be changed.*
>
> (1 Corinthians 15:51–52)

What a day that will be!

57

OVERCOMING PERSECUTION

Don Gossett

God's Word assures us that we will face persecution if we walk uprightly with the Lord. What do we do when we face persecution? As soldiers for Him, we can endure hard times.

> *All who desire to live godly in Christ Jesus will suffer persecution.* (2 Timothy 3:12 NKJV)

I've already shared how my father ridiculed me when I was a stuttering seventeen-year-old for wanting to preach. Ironically, when the Lord loosened my tongue so that I might speak with relative fluency, the same man encouraged me to use my speaking ability by pursuing a career as an auctioneer! Eventually, my father became a Christian, we reconciled, and he encouraged me in the ministry. Praise God!

A God-given vision is greater than all of man's persecutions. Neither my father's biting words, nor the fact that he didn't believe in me, could stop me. I had met Someone greater than my father.

My father's attitude was the first taste of the many persecutions to come. As the Lord of the harvest has sent me to evangelize in fifty-five nations, opposition has often been present. I have learned to overcome *"by the blood of the Lamb, and by the word of* [my] *testimony"* (Revelation 12:11).

To encourage you to face opposition and overcome it, I share with you four episodes of persecution from four different nations. The efforts to exterminate our crusades and to drive us out of these countries were great challenges. The hostility took many forms, from physical confrontations to verbal abuse to menacing crowds.

Bless them which persecute you: bless, and curse not.

(Romans 12:14)

I pray that as you read these true accounts, you will find faith to stand firm against the schemes of the evil one.

CHICAGO, ILLINOIS

During a crusade, I endeavored to minister to a man who was visiting the arena where I was preaching each day. After my first encounter with the man, he returned the following night with these sobering words: "When you shook my hand last night, something came over me, and I wanted to kill you."

As I continued to interact with this man, I worked to win him to Christ. Each time, however, he refused. A few days later, without any provocation on my part, he sprang upon me like an animal that has gone mad. His blows were severe. My face was bleeding, and I heard the man announce that he was going to cut out my eyes with his knife. I knew my life was on the line.

Boldly, I commanded the man, "Go down that street! Leave now, in the name of Jesus!"

The man left, only to appear at my hotel to further pursue his evil intentions against my life. The police arrested him and took him to jail.

When the man's trial took place, I was required to appear. He told the court that he had never laid a hand on me. When I testified, I described how the man had struck me three damaging blows. The man jumped up and shouted, "I only hit him twice!" Eventually, the court sentenced him to serve time in a facility for the criminally insane.

Jesus said, *"If they have persecuted me, they will also persecute you"* (John 15:20).

> *For though we walk in the flesh, we do not war after the flesh:... casting down imaginations, and every high thing that exalteth itself against the knowledge of God, and bringing into captivity every thought to the obedience of Christ.*
> (2 Corinthians 10:3, 5)

A key to overcoming persecution is *"casting down imaginations"* of any violent actions that have threatened your well-being. God's children should walk without fear.

GEORGETOWN, GUYANA

After arriving for a crusade organized by the churches of this South American nation, I was violently attacked by a member of a notorious mob known as the "Choke and Rob Gang." Their method of operation was to put piano wire around the throats of their victims and threaten to choke them if they did not give up their money. In our confrontation, my arm was cut, my watch was taken off of my arm, and I was warned of imminent danger at the third-class hotel where I was scheduled to stay.

After this traumatic experience, I announced that I was going to stay at a hotel with better security. When we arrived at the

Hotel Pegasus, I was informed that there were no rooms available. I told the clerk, "These pastors and I are going into your coffeehouse to have tea. When someone cancels his reservation, come and get me."

The clerk insisted, "Mr. Gossett, we are completely booked for many nights due to a convention in the city."

Still, the Holy Spirit gave me an inner witness: *A room will open for you.*

After about an hour, the same clerk came to me and said, "We do have a room for you, Mr. Gossett, but only for tonight. You will have to check out tomorrow."

It so happened that the Lord kept that room available for me the entire time I was in Guyana. In declaring that I would stay only in the hotel with the best security, I was walking in faith and wisdom.

A key to overcoming persecution is consulting the Lord about your problem and walking in His wisdom. He is a practical Father. With His instructions comes His provision. Walk in patience while waiting for His supply.

JERUSALEM, ISRAEL

A Christian film company from Seattle, Washington, invited me to make a documentary of the holiest places in Israel. At the famous Wailing Wall, while the camera was rolling and I was explaining the significance of this historic site, an irate Israeli man approached, cursing me and screaming. As he drew near, he angrily spat in my face. Several Jewish leaders nearby came to my defense and then apologized for the man's rude behavior. Even though the episode was defused within minutes, it was disconcerting to be the recipient of such hatred.

A key to overcoming persecution is not to allow hatred to lodge within your heart. Your overcoming faith works only if you walk in love, or by *"faith working through love"* (Galatians 5:6 NKJV).

BOMBAY, INDIA

For eighteen consecutive services, our crusade in India had been blessed with many people being delivered from sin, sickness, demons, and fear. Then, hell itself seemed to break loose as a band of several dozen radical Hindus stormed the crusade grounds, brandishing swords. They announced that they had come for "the North American evangelist who is turning many Hindus to Christianity."

I was that evangelist.

They cut the electrical power, plunging the athletic field into darkness and confusion. The local pastors used a bullhorn to try to settle the crowd. With my daughter and two Indian coworkers, we awaited directions from the local crusade leaders as to what we should do. I will never forget what happened in our hotel room later that evening. I read aloud from Acts the stirring accounts of the apostle Paul being stoned, imprisoned, and beaten. Yet Paul was not dismayed at all he had suffered. In fact, he later referred to it as *"our light affliction"* (2 Corinthians 4:17).

Later, when the pastors drove us in their jeep to the Bombay airport, they said they felt not unlike the Christians at Damascus as they lowered Paul in a basket over the wall to help him escape from those who wanted to kill him.

A key to overcoming persecution is walking with a consciousness that the Lord dwells within you. Walk confidently with the vision the Father has instilled within you.

A God-given vision is greater than all of mankind's persecutions. I experienced 2 Timothy 3:11:

Persecutions, afflictions,...what persecutions I endured: but out of them all the Lord delivered me.

Regardless of the opposition you face because of your faith, expect God's miracles for your life as you walk out His keys to overcoming persecution.

58

OVERCOMING LONELINESS

Don Gossett

One Saturday evening during my senior year of high school, the news broke over the radio that our town was experiencing flash flooding. Torrential waters were sweeping down from the canyon above our town, and the local river was overflowing its banks. Rapidly, the streets began to fill with water.

Among those wading through the knee-deep waters were my friend George and I. We were directly across from the post office when we met one of our high school friends, Bonnie Bjorklun, and her mother. We paused for a moment and talked with them about how "fun" the flood was.

We had hardly turned to go our own way when we heard a bloodcurdling scream. It was Mrs. Bjorklun, screaming as she gazed down at the sidewalk. Bonnie was nowhere in sight. As we rushed to the woman's side, she pointed down at an open manhole in the sidewalk. Bonnie had stepped into that hole and was gone! Only seconds before, we had been inches from that hole, which had been forced open by the rushing water but was almost invisible in the darkness.

Even though I held a Red Cross Lifesavers certificate, my ability to swim would not have helped in that enclosed drainage system, which was filled with surging floodwaters.

George and I accompanied Mrs. Bjorklun to her home, where we were joined by her son, Dale, another classmate from school. When I finally returned to the safety of my own home around one o'clock in the morning, I dropped to my knees for a long prayer session with the Lord. Even though I had accepted Christ as my Savior at the age of twelve, I had hardly allowed Him to become the Lord of my life. I felt so utterly alone that night. My parents had moved fifteen hundred miles away, and I would be spending most of my senior year of high school living alone.

That feeling of loneliness persisted in the days to come. I was a pallbearer at Bonnie's funeral. I was meeting God in prayer and studying His Word at every opportunity, primarily to seek His help in overcoming my desperate loneliness.

In my study, I discovered a Scripture passage that was to change my life as only God's Word can. It was Hebrews 13:5–6:

> *He hath said, I will never leave thee, nor forsake thee. So that we may boldly say, The Lord is my helper, and I will not fear what man shall do unto me.*

What an answer to my loneliness! No audible voice, no bright lights, just His pure Word giving me assurance.

Again on bended knee, I meditated on these facts:

- Jesus would be with me always, whatever the circumstances, good or bad.
- He would never leave me or forsake me.
- I could count on His presence wherever I went.

- His sweet presence and peace would always minister to my natural loneliness.

In His last words to His followers, Jesus promised, *"Lo, I am with you alway, even unto the end of the world"* (Matthew 28:20). This is not a careless promise from the lips of the Master of all creation.

He will be with us always.

59

OVERCOMING DISCOURAGEMENT

Don Gossett

When you feel discouraged, remember Jeremiah's experience. He was perhaps the most discouraged man in the entire Bible. First, he cried out, *"O Lord, thou hast deceived me, and I was deceived:...I am in derision daily, every one mocketh me"* (Jeremiah 20:7). He was so discouraged, he made a firm decision never to speak the Lord's name again. But Jeremiah had been nourished by the Word of God, and that indwelt Word began to take unusual effect. *"But his word was in mine heart as a burning fire shut up in my bones…"* (verse 9). The Word produced a *"burning fire"* within Jeremiah, such that he could remain quiet no longer.

That is what the Word will do in your life. It will create what I call "holy heartburn."

When you are discouraged, don't dare consult your feelings, your circumstances, or how things are going for you. Live only by the Word of God. This is how Jesus said to live a Christian life: *"Man shall not live by bread alone, but by every word that proceedeth* out of the mouth of God" (Matthew 4:4). You'll never be discouraged if you allow the Word to prevail and to have free course. (See Acts 19:20; 2 Thessalonians 3:1.)

When you are plagued by the memory of past sins, failures, mistakes, or disappointments, heed God's directive by *"forgetting those things which are behind, and reaching forth unto those things which are before"* (Philippians 3:13).

Satan specializes in robbing us of initiative by subtly reminding us of any dismal details from the past. Yet we can count on these glorious facts:

> *...the blood of Jesus Christ his Son cleanseth us from all sin.*
> (1 John 1:7)

> *As far as the east is from the west, so far hath he removed our transgressions from us.* (Psalm 103:12)

God specializes in giving each of us a new start. Accept the Lord's forgiveness of your past misdeeds, and be sure to forgive yourself, as well.

When you become bored with life, focus your attention on Jesus, God's incredible gift. Jesus Christ offers you abundant life (see John 10:10), unspeakable joy (see 1 Peter 1:8), the fullness of grace (see John 1:16), and peace that surpasses all human understanding (see Philippians 4:7).

When you are weary and life seems irksome, dull, and humdrum, act on this promise:

> *But they that wait upon the* LORD *shall renew their strength; they shall mount up with wings as eagles; they shall run, and not be weary; and they shall walk, and not faint.*
> (Isaiah 40:31)

The Bible has the answer for every problem. Study God's Word and discover His sure answers, which will help you to overcome anything you may face.

60

OVERCOMING UNFORGIVENESS

Don Gossett

If I forgive men and women of their trespasses against me, my heavenly Father will also forgive me my trespasses against Him. (See Matthew 6:14.) But if I refuse to forgive men and women of their trespasses against me, far more serious consequences than I had imagined will be mine: "Neither will your Father forgive your trespasses" (verse 15).

If I possess unforgiveness in my heart, regardless of the wrongdoings other people have committed against me, I open my heart to permit *"seven other spirits more wicked than* [unforgiveness]" to *"enter in, and dwell there"* (Luke 11:26). These seven other spirits are akin to unforgiveness but are even more wicked. I believe these spirits to be:

1. Resentment
2. Ill will
3. Grudges

4. Malice
5. Retaliation
6. Bitterness
7. Hatred

As I examine this list of seven other spirits more wicked than unforgiveness, I perceive that they are progressively destructive. How can I be delivered from unforgiveness? How can I resist these wrong spirits in Jesus's name, so that they must leave me?

Jesus defeated the devil by quoting God's Word. I shall likewise boldly declare God's Word against these vexing spirits, so that I might be totally liberated.

> *Be ye kind one to another, tenderhearted, forgiving one another, even as God for Christ's sake hath forgiven you.*
> (Ephesians 4:32)

Kindness is a fruit of the Spirit. When I practice kindness coupled with tenderheartedness, I am able to forgive all who have wronged me, even as God, for Christ's sake, has forgiven me.

> *Forbearing one another, and forgiving one another, if any man have a quarrel against any: even as Christ forgave you, so also do ye.* (Colossians 3:13)

God's Word is as practical as it is powerful. It shows me what to do, even if I should be involved in a petty quarrel.

> *Then Peter came to Him and said, "Lord, how often shall my brother sin against me, and I forgive him? Up to seven times?" Jesus said to him, "I do not say to you, up to seven times, but up to seventy times seven."* (Matthew 18:21–22 NKJV)

God's ability within me to forgive others is unlimited. I therefore possess not natural ability but supernatural ability whereby I can forgive others.

> *Herein is love, not that we loved God, but that he loved us, and sent his Son to be the propitiation for our sins. Beloved, if God so loved us, we ought also to love one another.*
>
> (1 John 4:10–11)

The greatest problems I encounter in life are usually "people problems." We live in a world where communications can break down, fellowship can be severed, and persecution and opposition can be our lot. But I know the secret: I have the ability to love with His love. I see others through eyes of God's tender love and compassion.

> *Let every man be swift to hear, slow to speak, slow to wrath: for the wrath of man worketh not the righteousness of God.*
>
> (James 1:19–20)

I refuse to speak unkindly against those who have wronged me. God enables me to forgive and to forget. These *"seven other spirits"* may often seek to regain entrance to my life, but I defiantly resist them in Jesus's name.

Some may say, "I would forgive others if they would only ask me for forgiveness." Whether they ask for forgiveness or not, in your heart of hearts, you can forgive and put all offenses under the blood of Jesus. As a believer in Jesus, you can forgive others. By the delivering power of the blood of Jesus, you are set free from those *"seven other spirits."*

61

THE POWER OF WORDS OF REBUKE

Don Gossett

In the synagogue there was a man, which had a spirit of an unclean devil, and cried out with a loud voice, saying, Let us alone; what have we to do with thee, thou Jesus of Nazareth? art thou come to destroy us? I know thee who thou art; the Holy One of God. And Jesus rebuked him, saying, Hold thy peace, and come out of him. And when the devil had thrown him in the midst, he came out of him, and hurt him not. And they were all amazed, and spake among themselves, saying, What a word is this! for with authority and power he commandeth the unclean spirits, and they come out.

(Luke 4:33–36)

In his version of this account, Mark added a vital question: "What new doctrine is this? for with authority commandeth he even the unclean spirits, and they do obey him" (Mark 1:27).

For many believers in our day, the idea of rebuking the devil with authority is a *"new doctrine."* It's new only because it is not practiced by the majority of Christians. Exercising the spoken word of rebuke is powerful.

Roberta Lashley has a remarkable testimony about the authority of the believer's rebuke, even when it is spoken by someone new to the faith. Roberta was seventeen when she was baptized in the Holy Spirit. Her baptism was evidenced by speaking in tongues. Being baptized in the Spirit is often a rapturous experience, as it was for Roberta. Caught up in the ecstasy of being filled with the Spirit, she forgot about the last bus that was headed toward her home. The delights of the fresh infilling were so joyful, Roberta didn't mind having to walk home that night.

The final leg of her hike was up part of Balk Knob Mountain, a steep grade leading to her home. Just as she began to ascend the mountain road, a car stopped. It was a common practice for people living on the mountain to offer rides to others who were walking. Roberta peered into the car and thought she recognized the driver as a neighbor. After getting into the car, she realized the man was a stranger.

As they approached her home, Roberta told the driver, "That's my home, right there," but the man didn't slow down. She repeated in a louder voice, "You just drove past my home. Please let me out now." But the man ignored her and sped up the mountain road.

By that point, it was no longer the blessed Holy Spirit controlling Roberta's emotions. There was an invader, the tormenting spirit of fear, vexing her. After the man stopped the car, he sneered, "I'm going to rape you, and then, I will kill you and drop your body down an abandoned mine shaft nearby. Nobody will ever know what happened to you."

Fear and panic were Roberta's unwelcome companions. But there was also a greater power: the mighty presence of the Holy

Spirit, the Helper who had been sent to her by Jesus. Roberta remembered missionaries from the Philippines who had visited her church and had related how they had used the "believer's rebuke" with great results. As the man began his evil actions, Roberta was endeavoring to recall the exact words the missionaries had used.

When the man came at her, Roberta spoke out: "I rebuke you in the name of Jesus Christ."

The impact of that spoken phrase of rebuke produced a startling reaction. The man pulled back quickly. Stammering, he said, "Rebuke? What does that mean?"

Roberta replied, "It means Jesus Christ has given me power over you, and you cannot harm me in any way."

The man started shaking. He grasped the steering wheel and began to scream, "I didn't know. I just didn't know." Then, he turned to Roberta and said, "I am really not a bad person. No, I'm not a bad person."

This must have sounded pathetic coming from a man who had just proclaimed that he was going to rape and kill a woman before tossing her body down an abandoned mine shaft!

The man continued his feeble defense. "I used to go to church," he said.

Then, the man restarted the car, backed up, and drove back down the mountain road. As he drove, Roberta quickly explained to him the love God had for him. He stopped in front of Roberta's home and let her out, where her mother was waiting at the front door.

In the account in Luke 4, Jesus rebuked the unclean spirit, and it came out, but nothing happened until He spoke those words of rebuke. Similarly, through her words, Roberta Lashley rebuked the devil's evil intentions through the wicked man, who was forbidden to do any harm to this woman. Nothing happened until

Roberta spoke those words of authority and rebuked the unclean power that possessed that man. What do you need to rebuke in your life? Do it now, by the authority of Jesus Christ.

62

DON'T BEAT THE DEVIL OUT; CAST HIM OUT!

Don Gossett

They were astonished at his doctrine: for his word was with power. And in the synagogue there was a man, which had a spirit of an unclean devil, and cried out with a loud voice, saying, Let us alone; what have we to do with thee, thou Jesus of Nazareth? art thou come to destroy us? I know thee who thou art; the Holy One of God. And Jesus rebuked him, saying, Hold thy peace, and come out of him. And when the devil had thrown him in the midst, he came out of him, and hurt him not. And they were all amazed, and spake among themselves, saying, What a word is this! for with authority and power he commandeth the unclean spirits, and they come out. And the fame of him went out into every place of the country round about. (Luke 4:32–37)

Jesus said, *"Hold thy peace, and come out of him,"* and the demon came out. Jesus spoke the words of authority that set the man free. But nothing happened until Jesus spoke!

In the Great Commission, as set forth in Mark 16, Jesus declared, *"And these signs shall follow them that believe; in my name shall they cast out devils"* (verse 17). It has been a sacred privilege to be used by the Lord to cast out demons and evil, unclean spirits, particularly in India, where the majority of the people worship idols, a practice that can lead to demon possession.

One time, while I was in Canada, a pastor friend of mine said, "Brother Gossett, I have a nineteen-year-old son named Ken. He is keenly interested in your ministry and would like to accompany you to some of your meetings." I consented and took Ken with me to several crusades.

At one meeting, the local pastors asked him to serve as an usher, which he was willing to do. A demon-possessed man came into the auditorium intent on disrupting the service. As he came charging up the aisle, cursing me with the vilest language, I motioned for the ushers to escort the man out of the meeting. As the ushers approached him, this demonized man turned on them and grabbed Ken, breaking his glasses and yanking the watch from his arm. Ken and another usher wrestled the man to the floor, pinning his arms down. Obviously agitated at the destruction of his glasses and watch, Ken began beating the man and screaming, "In the name of Jesus, come out!" From the front, I could hear "In the name of Jesus—" followed by the sound of Ken slugging the man.

I rushed to Ken and stopped him, saying, "That's not the way we do it. Jesus didn't say, 'Beat the devil out of people'; He said to cast out the devil in His name." I realized that my young friend needed more training on how to cast out demons and evil spirits.

For the weapons of our warfare are not carnal, but mighty through God to the pulling down of strong holds.
(2 Corinthians 10:4)

This is victory! The manifestations of the wicked, unfeeling devil can be so intense that one may feel tempted to use physical force. In effective spiritual warfare, however, it is operating in the anointing of the Holy Spirit that brings deliverance. *"And the yoke shall be destroyed because of the anointing"* (Isaiah 10:27).

63

LOVE NEVER FAILS

E. W. Kenyon

As we walk in love, we walk in the light of faith. As we walk in this light, we cannot fail. There is no failure in the life of love. Failure comes, instead, from selfishness.

As we walk in love, we walk in the light of God's Word. There is a continual sense of His protection and care.

> *The* LORD *is my light and my salvation; whom shall I fear? The* LORD *is the strength of my life; of whom shall I be afraid?*
> (Psalm 27:1)

As long as you walk in love, you are in the light. When you are walking in the light, you will not stumble. There is a fearless certainty about your life, about your decisions, about everything connected with your life.

You can confidently rest in the Word when it says,

> *Fear thou not; for I am with thee: be not dismayed; for I am thy God: I will strengthen thee; yea, I will help thee; yea, I will*

uphold thee with the right hand of my righteousness.

(Isaiah 41:10)

God is with you. God is in you. God is the strength of your life.

You cannot be sick.

You cannot be weak.

You cannot be ignorant of His will.

You know what His mind is because He imparts Himself and His ability to you. He whispers, *"Fear thou not; for I am with thee: be not dismayed; for I am thy God."*

What He means is, "I am your Father God, your Lover, your Protector, and your Caretaker."

It is easy to cast every care and anxiety upon Him. It is easy to rest in Him with a fearless joy.

I will strengthen thee; yea, I will help thee; yea, I will uphold thee with the right hand of my righteousness.

Never has righteousness been so beautiful.

God's righteousness is upholding us.

God's righteousness is making us fearless.

God's righteousness is making us conquerors, overcomers, and victors in every fight.

Now, we can put up a solid front before the world.

Now, we can enjoy His fullness.

We now know that we are who He says we are, and we rejoice in it.

64

ATTEMPT GREAT THINGS FOR GOD; EXPECT GREAT THINGS FROM GOD

Don Gossett

This was the lifetime motto of the London shoe cobbler William Carey. He is aptly remembered as the "father of modern missions."

William Carey was often called a foolish, impractical dreamer for studying foreign languages and reading the travel logs of Captain Cook. Many of those who knew him when he was a cobbler scoffed at the large map he kept on the wall of his workshop, which he used as he prayed for the nations of the world throughout the day.

Even after he became a minister, Carey was considered foolish for presenting the following topic for discussion at a ministers' conference: "Whether or Not the Great Commission Is Binding upon Us Today to Go and Teach All Nations." An older minister rebuked Carey, saying, "Sit down, young man. When God pleases to convert the heathen, He will do so without your aid or mine!"

Attempt Great Things for God; Expect Great Things from God

Carey was silenced for the moment but not stopped. He went on to become a pioneering missionary to India.

The same Holy Spirit dropped a love and a vision for India into my heart. For William Carey, to travel from England to India required much hardship. It took months of rough sea travel. I'm humble and grateful that God has sent me to India twenty-three times, each trip requiring about twenty-four hours each way on a large airplane.

> *Then Saul said to David, Blessed be thou, my son David: thou shalt both do great things, and also shalt still prevail.*
> (1 Samuel 26:25)

The Lord used William Carey mightily in India. Among other things, his translation of the Bible into various languages and dialects of India was a noble and lasting work.

While I hardly claim to have been used of the Lord in India as was Carey, I can relate to him in two respects: first, the action to translate for the people of India what I've written into the many languages there; second, the bitter opposition he experienced in going to that land.

The saddest memories I possess are the oppositions to my ministry I encountered in India. Some of those have already been mentioned in this book. It is heartbreaking to be so critically opposed when God knows the right motivations that compel me to preach all across that needy nation. While the tests have been severe, the victories have been far more glorious!

> *See to it that you complete the work you have received in the Lord.* (Colossians 4:17 NIV)

This holy command of Scripture is a vital part of my destiny. The King James Version says it even more pointedly: "*Take heed to the ministry which thou hast received in the Lord, that thou fulfil it.*" I deeply desire that you, too, would accomplish all that God has set for you to do on this earth. You have an appointed path.

You can spend your life any way you desire, but you can spend it only once. Years ago, I wrote down this quotation, generally attributed to Edward Everett Hale, and later, to Helen Keller:

> I am only one, but still I am one. I cannot do everything, but still I can do something;... I will not refuse to do the something that I can do.

Many people say that they will do great things for God—someday.

When I consider someone of strong vision overcoming discouragement and hardship to fulfill the vision of his or her ministry, I think of my dear friend Dennis White. Early in 2011, I was invited to preach at Dennis's church in Toronto. When he introduced me, he told the crowd about the forty-two years of ministry we had shared.

Dennis first invited me to Dominica in the 1960s. The open-air crusades we held in towns such as Roseau, Loubiere, Mahaut, and Delices are deeply embedded in my memory. I've often written about the experiences we shared: climbing five miles up a mountain each night for a crusade that reached hundreds with the gospel, being confronted by a snake on a mountain path, and the night I fell down a slippery mountain path.

After Dominica, Dennis and Esther White were led by God to invest fourteen years of their lives in Africa. On several occasions, Dennis invited me to fly to Nairobi, Kenya, where we shared the gospel together. God used Dennis to raise up large new churches in unreached areas. The life story of Dennis White is a powerful one of a man committed to the ripened harvest fields of the world. What a man of God! It has accurately been said that "when Dennis White opens his mouth, God fills it."

"MAKE NO LITTLE PLANS HERE!"

These were the words of my esteemed friend Oral Roberts. Brother Roberts lived out that motto as God used him to establish a fully accredited university with several graduate schools. Today, Oral Roberts University has thousands of alumni worldwide. The personal, handwritten letters that I received from Oral Roberts are among my most treasured possessions. Even today, they serve to encourage me.

Take the examples of these great men to heart. Don't exchange your life for far too little. Don't be afraid to think big. Don't be afraid to expect the miraculous. It was this kind of thinking that led me to go on radio in 1961, when I had no money, no supporters, and no one to encourage me. But the Lord gave me a vision that was "beyond the end of my nose." He showed me the nations of the world where I was to preach the gospel.

As I've mentioned before, I was called to serve the Lord when I was just seventeen years old. I began preaching in country Baptist churches when I was eighteen. I was told that I was too timid and shy to ever be of much use. Yet I learned to stand boldly on the Word of God and routinely affirmed, *"I can do all things through Christ who strengthens me"* (Philippians 4:13 NKJV). I memorized hundreds of Scriptures. As I spoke the Word of God aloud with confidence, the Holy Spirit developed a boldness within me that was foreign to my natural, negative personality.

The righteous are bold as a lion. (Proverbs 28:1)

What I spoke, I received: boldness in the form of confidence, fearlessness, courage, and the daring to do God's Word!

I've still got dreams and desires. Sometimes, they seem so big that I hardly know how or where to respond to make them come true. But we are attempting great things for God and expecting great things from Him!

You can be undaunted and do the same.

ABOUT THE AUTHORS

Dr. E. W. Kenyon

DR. E. W. KENYON (1867–1948) was born in Saratoga County, New York. At age nineteen, he preached his first sermon. He pastored several churches in New England and founded the Bethel Bible Institute in Spencer, Massachusetts. (The school later became the Providence Bible Institute when it was relocated to Providence, Rhode Island.) Kenyon served as an evangelist for over twenty years. In 1931, he became a pioneer in Christian radio on the Pacific Coast with his show *Kenyon's Church of the Air*, where he earned the moniker "The Faith Builder." He also began the New Covenant Baptist Church in Seattle. In addition to his pastoral and radio ministries, Kenyon wrote extensively.

Don Gossett

DON GOSSETT (1929–2014) served the Lord through full-time ministry for more than fifty years. Born again at the age of twelve, Don answered his call to the ministry just five years later and began by reaching out to his unsaved family members. Don apprenticed with many well-known evangelists, beginning with William Freeman, one of America's leading healing evangelists during the late 1940s. He also spent time with Raymond T. Richey, Jack Coe, and T. L. Osborn. Don's many writings have been translated into almost twenty languages and have exceeded twenty-five million in worldwide distribution. His daily radio show, launched in 1961, has been broadcast worldwide. Don raised five children with his first wife, Joyce, who died in 1991. In 1995, Don found lifelong love again and married Debra, an anointed teacher of the Word. They ministered worldwide and lived in British Columbia, Canada, and in Blaine, Washington State..